HISTORY'S STRANGEST MYSTERIES

CONTENTS

FOREWORD

The Puzzle is Real

The world is full of puzzles.

Not the kind you finish at the kitchen table. The kind you stumble across in a jungle. Or discover buried under ash. Or hidden in plain sight—like a message carved into stone that no one has ever been able to read.

That's what this book is about. Strange events. Lost civilizations. Forgotten codes. Every chapter is a case file, packed with real-world clues that still stump scientists and historians today.

Why did the ancient builders of the Great Pyramid use stones so massive we still don't know how they moved them? Why do maps from the 1500s show an ice-free coast of Antarctica—long before anyone had ever been there? Who carved giant stone heads on Easter Island, and how did they move them miles across the island without wheels?

We've found roads underwater. Skeletons buried in perfect circles. Lights in the sky that entire towns witnessed. And symbols deep inside pyramids that were sealed for thousands of years.

This isn't fiction. These things really happened. And we still don't have all the answers.

That's where you come in.

This book won't tell you what to believe. It won't hand you an easy solution. Instead, it gives you the clues— artifacts, locations, weird theories, and strange coincidences—so you can start asking better questions.

Follow the evidence. Weigh the facts. Question everything. Because maybe, just maybe, the people who built the pyramids, the ones who vanished from Roanoke, or whoever carved the Nazca Lines—they weren't trying to confuse us.

Maybe they were leaving a message.

And it's your job to figure out what it says.

Let the investigation begin.

STONEHENGE

What was Stonehenge created for?

How were such massive stones
moved and constructed?

How did the creators of Stonehenge
learn the astronomy necessary to
align the stones with celestial events?

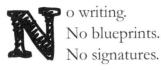o writing.
No blueprints.
No signatures.

Just two dozen rocks the size of delivery trucks, planted in a near-perfect circle on a windswept field in England.

Some of these boulders were dragged—yes, dragged—over 150 miles. Across hills. Through rivers. Without wheels. Without roads. Without iron tools.

No one knows who built it. No one knows how. And no one knows why.

That's why we're here.

It's called Stonehenge. And it's been confusing people for over 5,000 years. Even the name is weird: "henge" comes from an old word meaning "hanging." Hanging stones? Doesn't exactly clear things up.

What we do know is this: it was built before the Great Pyramid. Before written history in Britain. Before glass, concrete, or the idea of a "building permit."

Whoever built it had no books, no metal, no machines. But they had a plan—and an obsession. The stones weren't tossed down like leftovers. They were shaped and placed with extreme precision. The giant uprights are locked together by carved joints, like stone puzzle pieces. The horizontal lintels up top aren't straight—they're curved, bent just enough to complete a perfect circle in the air.

This wasn't a guess. This was geometry.

And that brings us to the first clue.

The sun.

Once a year, on the longest day—summer solstice—the sun rises and sends a beam of light slicing through the circle, hitting one lonely rock called the Heel Stone. On the shortest day—winter solstice—the sunset drops neatly between two giant uprights on the opposite side. The sun moves. The stones do not. Which means someone tracked those solar rhythms and built this place to match.

That's not an accident. It's a design.

Was it a calendar? A solar temple? A way to count the seasons or call the sun back from winter? Maybe. But a calendar can't explain what's buried here.

Which brings us to clue number two.

Bones.

Under and around the circle, archaeologists have uncovered cremated human remains—burned and buried over 5,000 years ago. Some were local. Others came from far across the island. A few were children. Dozens of burials, carefully arranged. This wasn't a random graveyard. It was ceremonial.

Some experts think Stonehenge was a place of healing. A prehistoric hospital. The smaller "bluestones," which came from the Preseli Hills in distant Wales, were believed to have special power. Maybe people traveled from miles away to bring their sick, their injured, their dying—to be cured, or to be honored.

Even today, visitors leave flowers, crystals, and notes in the cracks between stones. The energy still draws people in.

But the third clue suggests something even stranger.

Roast beef.

Well—cattle bones, to be exact. Split bones, butcher marks, ash pits, broken pottery, and charred wood. Signs of enormous winter feasts. Hundreds of people gathering at once, lighting fires, sharing drinks, roasting whole animals.

This wasn't just a sacred spot. It was a party zone.

A place of celebration, not just silence. A winter festival on sacred ground.

So what do we make of it? A temple. A clock. A graveyard. A hospital. A dance floor.

Maybe it was all of those. Maybe it changed over time. The earliest parts of the site go back to 3000 BCE, but the full monument wasn't completed until centuries later. Each generation may have added to it, shaped it, reinterpreted its purpose—without ever knowing what the original builders had in mind.

And then there's the question no one can answer: how did they move the stones?

The biggest ones—called sarsens—came from about 20 miles away. Each weighs as much as four elephants. The smaller bluestones came from 150 miles off, across rivers, forests, and rugged terrain. No wheels. No oxen. Just ropes, sleds, and people.

They might've rolled them over logs. Or floated them down rivers. Or dragged them in the snow. Every theory is difficult. And none explain the accuracy.

This wasn't sloppy. This was exact.

And it wasn't the only monument. Satellite scans have revealed hidden pits, timber posts, burial mounds, and roads buried beneath the fields around Stonehenge. It was the center of something bigger—a sacred zone, a prehistoric capital of mystery.

But no one left a message. No instructions. No answers.

Just questions.

The deeper we dig, the weirder it gets.

Stonehenge doesn't explain itself: it just dares you to keep looking.

ATLANTIS

Did Atlantis ever exist? Was it just a
story made up by Plato?

Where was it, and if it was real,
what made it sink into the sea?

Atlantis was never meant to be history.

The first time it was mentioned—in the writings of the philosopher Plato—it was a warning. A tale about pride, power, and a city swallowed by the sea.

But then people started looking for it.

Over the centuries, explorers, archaeologists, and treasure hunters have searched for a sunken city that fits Plato's description: beyond the Pillars of Hercules, rich in gold, full of strange animals, and gone in a single day.

So far, no one's found it. But the clues? They keep showing up.

Ruins beneath the ocean. Maps with vanished islands. Earthquakes in the right places. Even possible locations scattered across the world—from the Mediterranean to Antarctica.

Is Atlantis a memory of a real place? A twisted version of a natural disaster? Or just a myth people want to believe?

Let's weigh the evidence and see what still rises from the deep.

Plato's story is our starting point. He wrote of an island nation larger than Libya and Asia combined, located beyond the Pillars of Heracles—what we now call the Strait of Gibraltar. Atlantis, he said, existed 9,000 years before his time. It was powerful, wealthy, and technologically advanced. Then, in a single night, it was gone—swallowed by the sea.

Most historians dismissed the tale as fiction. But in the 19th century, a U.S. congressman named Ignatius Donnelly challenged that view. In 1882, he published Atlantis: The Antediluvian World, a book that exploded in popularity.

Donnelly argued that Atlantis wasn't a legend. It was the source of all ancient civilizations. He claimed the myths, languages, religions, and architecture of Egypt, Mesopotamia, and even the Americas could be traced back to this sunken empire. He wasn't an archaeologist—but his theories, however shaky, captured imaginations across the globe.

As speculation spread, so did the hunt.

In the 20th century, Atlantis became a global obsession. Scholars, divers, mystics, and scientists all claimed to be closing in on the truth. British researcher E.A. Spence pointed to the Moroccan coast, arguing that trade winds and ancient shipping routes matched Plato's clues. His theory didn't stick—but it started a wave of geographic guessing.

In 1968, divers near Bimini Island in the Bahamas discovered a strange underwater formation: a flat path of large limestone blocks beneath the waves. It looked like a road—or the remnants of a massive stone dock. Dubbed the Bimini Road, it sparked a frenzy. Was it a natural formation, or the edge of a lost city?

Meanwhile, a more grounded theory took shape in the Aegean Sea.

Archaeologists on the island of Santorini—ancient Thera—unearthed the remains of a sophisticated Bronze Age civilization buried in volcanic ash. Around 1600 BCE, a massive eruption had destroyed the city and caused tsunamis across the region. The eruption matched many details from Plato's account: a sudden catastrophe, advanced buildings, and a coastal empire lost overnight.

This theory points to the Minoan civilization as a possible inspiration for Atlantis. But there's a problem—Thera isn't beyond the Pillars of Heracles. So the search continued.

Some turned their attention to the Sahara Desert. There lies the Richat Structure, a huge, circular landform in Mauritania that eerily matches Plato's description of concentric rings of land and water. Though it's inland today, some believe it was once connected to the ocean. Its shape is hard to ignore.

And then came the Antarctica theory.

A group of researchers proposed that thousands of years ago, a rapid pole shift pushed a lush, inhabited region into the frozen wasteland we know today. Maps like the 16th-century Piri Reis chart—which seems to depict an ice-free Antarctic coastline—have been offered as potential proof. If true, Atlantis could be trapped under miles of ice.

In the 1990s, Russian sonar scans of the Mid-Atlantic Ridge revealed unusual shapes and ridges along the seafloor. Some looked man-made. Others resembled pyramid-like structures. None have been confirmed. But they added fuel to the fire.

Meanwhile, ancient texts offered new possibilities. Some researchers believe Egyptian priests told the tale to the Greek lawmaker Solon, who passed it down to Plato. If true, Atlantis might be a memory passed through generations—of a real disaster, distorted over time, but never fully forgotten.

Whether it's volcanic islands, desert rings, or icy continents, every theory adds another layer. And every layer brings more questions.

Atlantis may be a myth. But it's a myth with evidence scattered across oceans, deserts, and bookshelves.

And like all the best mysteries, it refuses to stay submerged.

THE GREAT PYRAMIDS OF GIZA

How did the ancient Egyptians move those huge stones to build such amazing structures?

How did they cut the stones so perfectly that the edges are almost invisible to the naked eye?

They didn't have cranes. They didn't have wheels. They didn't even have iron tools.

And yet the ancient Egyptians built the Great Pyramid out of more than 2 million limestone blocks—some weighing over 70 tons. The joints between the stones are razor-tight. You couldn't slip a credit card between them. The corners align almost perfectly with the four cardinal directions. The base is level to within less than an inch—even across hundreds of feet.

So how did they do it?

No blueprints survive. No records explain the construction process. Just theories—ramps, pulleys, levers, sweat, and genius. Some say it's proof of lost knowledge. Others believe it was just brilliance and brute force.

But the closer you look, the weirder it gets.

Because the Great Pyramid wasn't the end result of centuries of improving pyramid tech—it was the starting point. What came after it got worse. Later pyramids were smaller, messier, less precise. Many collapsed. Some were never finished. It's like the builders of Khufu's pyramid knew something that no one else did—or had access to techniques that were later lost.

How could they go from near-perfection… to rubble?

Some say the Great Pyramid was a one-time national obsession, an all-out campaign of labor and faith. Others think the knowledge was deliberately hidden. Or lost in a collapse. Or maybe never fully understood in the first place.

Whatever the case, the Great Pyramid stood alone. Silent. Sealed.

By the time the Greeks and Romans came along, no one even knew how to get in.

That changed in 820 CE, when Caliph Al-Ma'mun arrived from Baghdad with a team of workers, tools, and orders to crack it open.

With no entrance in sight, his crew picked a spot and started digging. Day after day, they hacked at stone that hadn't been touched in over 3,000 years—until they struck something: a hidden passage.

Al-Ma'mun expected treasure. Instead, he found strange tunnels, empty rooms, angled ceilings, and polished floors. No gold. No instructions. Just stonework so exact it felt unnatural. In his time, many believed the pyramid held secrets from before the Great Flood—knowledge from prophets or beings beyond this world.

He didn't find proof. But he reopened the mystery.

For centuries after, travelers returned from Giza with wild theories: giants, magicians, survivors of Atlantis. With no way to read the ancient writing found elsewhere in Egypt, the pyramid became a blank page. People filled it with whatever they wanted.

That changed in 1799, when a French soldier found the Rosetta Stone—one message written in Greek, Demotic, and Egyptian hieroglyphs. Using it, French scholar Jean-François Champollion cracked the ancient language in 1822. For the first time in over a thousand years, the Egyptians could speak again.

Suddenly, the pyramid had a name: Khufu. A Fourth Dynasty pharaoh. The graffiti found inside—red paint scribbled by ancient workers—matched his name. The mystery got smaller. But not by much.

In the 1800s, explorers crawled through clogged tunnels and blasted into hidden chambers. They found more clues: sloped shafts pointing at stars, blocks so perfectly carved they fit together like LEGO.

Later archaeologists, like George Reisner, brought science to the site—mapping tombs, collecting tools, and proving that these weren't slave-built tombs. These were the coordinated efforts of skilled labor crews, supported by the state, working with care and precision.

Still, some parts remained off-limits.

In 1993, a small robot called Upuaut entered one of the pyramid's narrowest shafts. It crept into the dark and came to a stop at a limestone door—fitted with two copper handles. Behind it? Unknown.

The door remains unopened.

Then in 2017, scientists used cosmic ray detectors to scan the pyramid without touching it. What they found stunned everyone: a massive hidden chamber, over 100 feet long, sitting above the Grand Gallery. It wasn't on any map. No one had ever been inside.

They called it the Big Void.

What's it for? A storage space? A construction trick? Something ceremonial? No one knows. But the fact remains: 4,500 years later, this building still hides things. Still surprises us. Still won't give up its full story.

The Great Pyramid wasn't just a tomb. It was a message—cut in stone, sealed in mystery, and built to last forever.

EASTER ISLAND

How did the people of Easter
Island carve and move such
gigantic stone statues?

What tools did they use?

A thousand miles from anywhere, a triangle of volcanic rock rises from the Pacific.

It's just 14 miles long and 7 miles wide—barely a dot on the map. But scattered across this lonely island are nearly 900 stone statues, each weighing tons. Some stand taller than a house. Others lie half-buried, unfinished or toppled.

They have long ears, heavy brows, long noses. Their backs to the sea. Their blank eyes once held coral.

They're called moai.

But what are they for? Who carved them? And how did an isolated group of people—cut off from the rest of the world—build one of the greatest sculptural achievements in human history? ·

Let's follow the clues.

The islanders call their home Rapa Nui. To outsiders, it became known as Easter Island after Dutch explorers arrived on Easter Sunday, 1722. What they found shocked them: towering stone heads, empty fields, and a population far smaller than expected. The trees were gone. The land looked stripped. Something had happened—but what?

The moai were the first clue.

Each one had been carved from volcanic tuff, mostly from a single quarry called Rano Raraku. Some statues were over 30 feet tall. Others weighed more than 80 tons. But the real mystery wasn't how they were made. It was how they were moved.

No wheels. No metal tools. No draft animals.

Yet the statues had been transported miles across rough terrain.

Some theorized the islanders used logs to roll the statues. But the island today has almost no trees. In fact, pollen samples show that it once had palm forests—dense, tall, and now gone. What happened?

One theory: the people of Rapa Nui cut down their forests to move statues. Over generations, the trees vanished. Without trees, soil eroded. Crops failed. Conflict broke out. The culture that once built statues turned inward. Civil war erupted. Statues were toppled. The island collapsed.

It's a dramatic story. Some call it "ecocide"—a warning for the future.

But new clues suggest something different.

Recent archaeological studies show that moai weren't symbols of ego—they were symbols of care. Many were placed near freshwater sources. Their eyes, once filled with white coral, always looked inland, never out to sea.

Some researchers now believe the statues were part of a spiritual system tied to agriculture. The ancestors, embodied in the moai, watched over gardens and protected water.

Another clue: tool marks.

Stone tools used to carve the moai were made of basalt and closely match tools found across Polynesia. That links Rapa Nui to a much larger story—the spread of voyagers across the Pacific. The people who settled Rapa Nui came from the west, likely from the Marquesas or Mangareva, navigating thousands of miles in double-hulled canoes using stars, birds, currents, and cloud patterns.

They brought sweet potatoes from South America and chickens from Asia.

Their arrival—sometime between 800 and 1200 CE—turned the island into a world of its own.

So what happened?

Yes, the trees disappeared. But pollen records suggest it wasn't just humans. A type of rat, brought on boats, may have eaten the seeds of the native palms, stopping regrowth. And diseases and slavery brought by outsiders in the 1700s and 1800s wiped out much of the population.

By the time Europeans arrived, Rapa Nui had already been broken—not only by internal struggles but by contact.

And yet, the people survived.

The statues still stood. Some still do.

And the secrets of how they were moved? Islanders say the statues "walked." That might sound like myth—until researchers tested it. Using ropes and teams, they rocked the statues forward, side to side. The statues swayed like massive stone penguins.

They really could walk.

So what do we have?

A tiny island. Dozens of unfinished statues. A lost forest. Oral traditions. A culture that rose, adapted, and nearly vanished—only to endure.

The moai aren't just relics. They're records.

Each one holds a puzzle piece.

Not just about how humans shape stone—but how belief, environment, and survival are all tied together.

Some mysteries remain. Why were some statues never finished? Were the toppled ones destroyed in anger—or just abandoned? And what of the rongorongo tablets—wooden planks carved with a script no one can read?

No one has cracked the code.

Not yet.

But one thing is clear:

Easter Island isn't a cautionary tale of failure.

It's a clue-filled story of resilience.

A message carved in stone, waiting to be understood.

THE SPHINX

Who carved the Great Sphinx, and why?

How did people before the ancient Egyptians create such an enormous statue?

Could there be secret rooms or treasures hidden beneath it?

It's taller than a six-story building. Carved from a single ridge of limestone.

The Great Sphinx of Giza has no inscriptions, no builder's name, no clear purpose. It just stares—silent and still—across 4,000 years of blowing sand.

But the real mystery is under the surface.

Some stones in its nearby enclosure are cut so precisely that modern saws would struggle to match them. The body shows signs of erosion—deep, rounded grooves that some believe were carved by thousands of years of rain.

That would make the Sphinx older than the pyramids themselves.

Too old. According to most textbooks, it shouldn't be there.

So who carved it?

When?

And why?

Archaeologists debate the evidence. Geologists argue about water damage. Theories clash like chisel against stone.

One thing is certain: The Sphinx isn't just a statue. It's a question.

Let's get closer—and see what it's still trying to say.

The Sphinx sits at the edge of the Giza plateau, just southeast of the Great Pyramid. Its body stretches over 240 feet long. Its paws reach forward as if mid-pounce. Its face—weathered but still regal—watches the rising sun.

No writing identifies its builder. No tomb lies beneath it. No blueprint was ever found. And yet it may be the oldest surviving monument in Egypt.

Mainstream archaeologists believe the Sphinx was carved around 2500 BCE, during the reign of Pharaoh Khafre. They argue that the Sphinx's face resembles statues of Khafre and that its location next to his pyramid connects the two.

But not everyone agrees.

Some scholars and geologists believe the evidence tells a different story.

One clue lies in the erosion. The body of the Sphinx, especially inside the surrounding enclosure, is heavily weathered. But the marks aren't sharp or wind-cut like other monuments in the area. They're smooth. Curved. The kind of erosion caused by heavy, repeated rainfall.

And that's a problem—because Giza hasn't seen serious rainfall in over 5,000 years.

To some, this suggests that the Sphinx is far older than Khafre's time. Older than the pyramids. Older, possibly, than the dynastic Egyptian civilization itself.

Geologist Robert Schoch is one of the best-known voices behind the rain erosion theory. In the 1990s, he examined the Sphinx and concluded that it must date back to at least 7000 BCE—if not earlier. That would place its construction in a mysterious, poorly understood prehistoric period known as the Neolithic.

But who would've carved it back then?

That's where the theories get stranger.

Some believe an unknown civilization predating the Egyptians left the Sphinx behind. Others think it was built by early Egyptians whose knowledge of stonework and astronomy was far more advanced than we give them credit for. A few even suggest the statue was originally a lion—only later recarved into a human face by later pharaohs.

There's another clue worth noting: the head looks too small.

The proportions are off. The body is massive, powerful, feline. But the head is narrow and upright, like it was carved after the body—or reshaped from something else.

Was the original face weathered away? Or was it altered on purpose to fit a ruler's image? No one knows.

Beneath the Sphinx, more questions hide. Seismic surveys in the 1990s revealed possible chambers and cavities under the statue. Some researchers believe these could be natural cracks. Others think they're manmade—rooms or passages that haven't been opened in thousands of years.

Egyptian authorities have long restricted excavation beneath the Sphinx, which only adds to the speculation. Some call it science. Others call it secrecy.

There's also the issue of alignment.

The Sphinx faces directly east, toward the rising sun on the spring equinox. Some researchers argue this points to a connection with astronomy. A few even claim the statue lines up with the constellation Leo—as it would have appeared around 10,500 BCE, a time some link with ancient global cataclysms and the lost city of Atlantis.

That's a long leap. But the Sphinx invites leaps. It's too strange not to wonder.

Despite decades of digging, scanning, and debate, the Sphinx remains frustratingly quiet. Its paws rest on dry stone. Its back is weathered and patched. Its eyes are unreadable.

And yet it endures.

It has no story written on its walls, no treasure buried beneath it. But it has outlasted empires. It has survived earthquakes, looters, and the slow, steady grinding of time.

And it still holds its secrets.

Maybe it was Khafre. Maybe it was someone far older. Maybe it was both—one builder starting something, another reshaping it.

Whatever the truth, the Sphinx remains the world's most famous riddle carved in stone.

KING ARTHUR

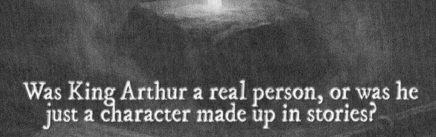

Was King Arthur a real person, or was he
just a character made up in stories?

Where was Camelot, the famous castle
where King Arthur and his knights lived?

tart with the name: Arthur.

It appears in old poems, battle lists, and dusty manuscripts—but never quite the same way twice. No birth record. No burial site. No statue carved in his image. Just whispers of a war leader who may have ruled in the shadows between the fall of the Roman Empire and the rise of medieval kings.

So where do you begin?

You start with the clues.

One of the oldest comes from a monk named Nennius, writing around 800 CE. In his book *Historia Brittonum*, he mentions a brave commander named Arthur who led the Britons in twelve battles. It's not much—but it's something. No mention of Camelot. No mention of Excalibur. Just a name, a sword, and a string of victories.

Was that the real Arthur?

Three hundred years later, another clue appears.

A man named Geoffrey of Monmouth writes *The History of the Kings of Britain*. It's part myth, part history, and all legend. Suddenly, Arthur isn't just a warrior—he's a king. He wears a golden crown. He builds a shining court called Camelot. He commands an army of loyal knights. Geoffrey's account spreads like wildfire. But historians aren't sure if he made it up or built it from older sources we no longer have.

Then there's the sword.

Two swords, actually. In one version, Arthur pulls a blade from a stone. In another, the Lady of the Lake lifts Excalibur from the water. Same king. Different swords. Which came first? And which, if any, were based on something real?

The mystery deepens.

In medieval romances, new details appear: the Round Table. Lancelot. Guinevere. Merlin. Morgan le Fay. And the most sacred quest of all—the Holy Grail.

But as the legends grow more magical, the real-world trail grows cold.

So what do modern historians think?

Some believe Arthur was based on a real warrior who lived around 500 CE, after the Roman legions left. He may have fought Saxon invaders. Maybe he wasn't a king—but a general, trying to hold Britain together.

Others think Arthur was never one man at all.

Instead, he may be a blend of several heroes—each with his own legend—combined over time into one mythical figure. A patchwork king stitched from Britain's past.

Or maybe Arthur was never real in any historical sense. Not a person, but a symbol. A hero dreamed up to inspire people in dark times. A story that said: "We had a golden age once—and maybe we can again."

The more you dig, the more questions you find.

Was Camelot real? Some say it was based on Cadbury Castle in Somerset, an ancient hill fort. Others say it's entirely fictional—a symbol of the perfect court.

And Avalon? Some link it to Glastonbury, where monks claimed to find Arthur's bones. Most scholars believe they faked it to attract pilgrims.

Even the Round Table leaves a trail. One hangs in Winchester, England—huge, wooden, painted with the names of knights. But it was built a thousand years too late.

And still, people search.

Because Arthur's story is full of clues—not the kind that lead to one truth, but that spiral out like the table itself. A cycle of myth and memory, hope and history, retold for a thousand years.

THE
KNIGHTS
TEMPLAR

What ancient secrets did the Knights
Templar really keep?

How did they gather so much wealth and
power, only to lose it all in the blink of an eye?

They started as poor knights—barely a dozen of them—swearing vows of poverty, chastity, and obedience.

By the time they disappeared, they were one of the most powerful and mysterious forces in Europe.

They had castles on nearly every border. A private fleet of ships. A vast banking network. Secret rituals. Hidden tunnels. Whispered symbols carved in stone.

And then, just like that, they were gone.

In a single day, their leaders were arrested. Their assets were seized. Their order was destroyed. Their final secrets went underground—if they ever made it out at all.

They were called the Knights Templar.

And some believe they never really disappeared.

The Knights Templar were founded in 1119, in the aftermath of the First Crusade. Their original mission was simple: protect Christian pilgrims traveling to the Holy Land. The road from Europe to Jerusalem was long and dangerous. Robbers, mercenaries, and bandits waited in the shadows. So these knights—armed monks, really—offered protection.

But their name said more: The Poor Fellow-Soldiers of Christ and of the Temple of Solomon.

That last part—Temple of Solomon—would stick.

Because the Templars weren't just warriors. They were based on the Temple Mount in Jerusalem, a site believed to hold ancient Biblical secrets. And not long after settling there, things started to change.

The order grew fast. Money poured in. Land. Donations. Favor from kings and popes.

They began to build massive stone fortresses, not just in the Holy Land but across Europe. Each was built to the same general plan: thick walls, hidden rooms, narrow stairwells, escape tunnels. Their buildings had strange carvings—two knights riding one horse, geometric symbols, circular chapels with no clear origin.

They wore white cloaks marked with a red cross. They trained constantly. They rarely spoke.

But their influence wasn't just military. It was financial.

The Templars invented a system that worked like early banking. A pilgrim could deposit money at one Templar commandery in Europe and receive a coded document. Once in Jerusalem, he could exchange that slip for the same amount—minus a fee.

It was safer than traveling with gold. And it made the Templars incredibly wealthy.

They financed kings. Held debt. Guarded treasure. Transported secret cargo on private ships.

That's when the rumors began.

Some said they discovered something beneath the Temple Mount—scrolls, relics, or even the Ark of the Covenant. Others believed they guarded the Holy Grail, the cup said to have been used by Jesus at the Last Supper.

The order had become too powerful. Too rich. Too secretive.

And some people wanted them gone.

On Friday the 13th, 1307, the trap was sprung.

King Philip IV of France—deeply in debt to the Templars—ordered the arrest of every Templar in his kingdom. Their Grand Master, Jacques de Molay, was taken. So were hundreds of others.

They were accused of heresy. Devil worship. Secret oaths. Spitting on the cross. No solid evidence was ever presented. But under torture, many confessed to whatever the inquisitors wanted.

Some later took it back. Others didn't get the chance.

Over the next seven years, the order was dismantled. Castles burned. Leaders executed. De Molay was burned at the stake in 1314. Legend says he cursed the king and the pope as the flames rose.

Within a year, both were dead.

The Pope officially dissolved the order, but he didn't erase it. Templar property was transferred to the Knights Hospitaller, another military order—but not everything was accounted for.

The Templars' massive treasure? Gone. Their fleet of ships? Gone. Their secret documents and artifacts? Vanished.

The silence was suspicious.

That's when the theories began to multiply.

Some believe the surviving Templars went underground, blending into other organizations. Others say they fled to Scotland or Switzerland. A few connect them to Freemasonry, claiming the symbols and rituals were passed down in secret.

Strange Templar carvings have been found in remote places—Scotland, Portugal, even North America. Some say they were here before Columbus.

Is any of it true? No one knows for sure. But the clues are real. Strange stone chapels with spiral symbols. Letters from kings referencing secret cargo. Mysterious tunnels under former Templar strongholds.

And always—the red cross, the double-rider emblem, and the sense that someone left in a hurry… with something worth hiding.

So who were the Templars, really? Holy warriors? Bankers? Treasure keepers? Guardians of a lost secret?

Whatever truth they carried, they didn't give it up easily.

THE
GREAT
FLOOD

Did the Great Flood really happen, or is it just
a story that has been told for ages?

If it did happen, what could have caused so
much water to cover the Earth?

From the Bible to the Epic of Gilgamesh, from remote Pacific islands to high Andean peaks—ancient stories tell of a time when the sky broke open and the oceans rose.

Whole cities vanished. Mountains became islands. A few survivors floated on rafts, boats, or hollowed-out logs, watching their world disappear beneath the waves.

For years, people called it myth.

But the more scientists study the past, the more patterns they find—flood layers in the soil, sunken ruins off the coastlines, and sudden sea level spikes that match the stories.

Could all these legends be echoes of the same event?

Was there a single flood—or many?

And why do so many stories share the same details?

The answers might lie in geology, in myth, or in both.

Let's sift through the layers, map the high-water marks, and follow the trail of the flood that no one forgot.

It started, oddly enough, with a damaged clay tablet in the British Museum. Pulled from the ruins of Nineveh, it sat untouched for years—just one of thousands recovered from the ancient library of King Ashurbanipal. Then came the breakthrough: a description of a man warned by a god, building a boat, saving animals, and surviving a flood that destroyed the world.

The text wasn't written in Hebrew. It wasn't from the Bible. It was older—Mesopotamian.

Suddenly, one of history's most sacred stories had an earlier version. And once that connection was made, it sparked a bigger question: if the flood appeared in Mesopotamian myth long before the Book of Genesis, could it be based on a real disaster?

The flood story wasn't unique to Mesopotamia. Nearly every corner of the world had one. In India, China, Greece, and even the Americas, tales tell of divine warnings, giant waves, floating arks, and life beginning again after everything is washed away. Coincidence? Or memory passed from generation to generation?

In the 1920s, British archaeologist Leonard Woolley began digging in the ancient city of Ur, deep in the soil of southern Iraq. Layer after layer revealed normal urban life—until one level, ten feet thick, showed nothing but silt. No artifacts. No buildings. Just water-laid clay. And beneath it? More human remains, from an earlier time.

Something had drowned the city and buried it. Not the whole world, perhaps—but enough to change everything for the people who lived there.

Far from Iraq, other flood clues began to surface.

In eastern Washington state, geologist J Harlen Bretz puzzled over a strange, scarred landscape. Massive ripple marks lined the ground. Boulders the size of trucks sat on flat plains. Rivers couldn't have carved it. Rain couldn't have done it. The only explanation? A flood—a massive one.

Eventually, Bretz's wild theory was proven right. Thousands of years ago, Glacial Lake Missoula was held back by an enormous ice dam. When that dam broke, it unleashed more water than all the world's rivers combined. The flood tore across the land again and again, reshaping it with every burst.

And it wasn't the only one.

In 1997, geologists William Ryan and Walter Pitman studied sediments in the Black Sea and found something strange. Around 5600 BCE, seawater from the Mediterranean had surged through the Bosporus Strait, flooding a huge freshwater basin in what's now eastern Europe. In months, over 60,000 square miles of land vanished under saltwater.

The sea didn't rise—it exploded inward.

If people lived along those ancient shores—and evidence suggests they did—they would've seen their homes, crops, and villages vanish beneath the waves. The memory of such an event wouldn't disappear. It would be told and retold, carried inland with every survivor.

In 1999, explorer Robert Ballard—the man who discovered the Titanic—sent a robotic submersible into the Black Sea. He wasn't chasing a legend. He wanted evidence. What he found, in the deep, oxygen-free water, was a structure: wooden beams, a buried wall, something man-made. People had lived there before the flood. Which meant the story wasn't just imagined.

It was remembered.

Today, the search continues. Scientists use satellite images, ground-penetrating radar, and sediment cores to scan for more flood evidence across the globe—from lost coastlines in India to sudden sea-level shifts in the Americas. Some look for tsunami deposits. Others follow fossilized tree lines now deep underwater. But all of them are asking the same thing:

Could humanity's oldest story come from something real?

Maybe not one flood, but many. Disasters that shook entire regions, split generations, and left behind survivors who turned their pain into stories that echoed across cultures.

And those stories are still with us.

Buried in clay. Sung in myth. Etched in stone.

Waiting for the next clue.

THE ARK
OF THE
COVENANT

Where did the Ark of the Covenant
disappear to?

What was inside, besides the stone
tablets with the Ten Commandments?

old-covered. Carried on poles. Guarded so closely that touching it meant death.

The Ark of the Covenant was the most sacred object in ancient Israel—a golden chest said to hold the stone tablets of the Ten Commandments. It was kept behind veils. Carried into battle. Blamed for plagues, victories, and terrifying power.

Then it disappeared.

Not stolen. Not destroyed. Just... gone.

It vanished from the historical record sometime after the First Temple was destroyed. No one wrote down where it was hidden—or why. That silence only made the legend grow louder.

Over the centuries, the clues have pointed everywhere: Ethiopia. Jerusalem. A cave. A vault. A mountain.

Every few decades, someone claims they've found it. Every time, it slips away again.

If it ever existed at all... it hasn't stopped hiding.

Let's retrace the trail, examine what's real, and follow the last known footsteps of the world's most wanted relic.

According to the Hebrew Bible, the Ark wasn't just sacred—it was designed by God Himself.

The story goes like this: After the Israelites escaped slavery in Egypt, they camped at the base of Mount Sinai. That's where Moses climbed the mountain, disappeared into smoke and thunder, and returned with something strange—stone tablets engraved with ten laws.

But these weren't just any tablets. They were said to be carved by "the finger of God."

To protect them, God gave Moses blueprints for a box— the Ark. It had to be made of acacia wood and covered entirely in gold. It had a lid called the Mercy Seat, with two golden angels (cherubim) on top. And no one was allowed to touch it directly—only the priests could carry it, using poles that slid through rings on the sides.

Inside the Ark?

- The two stone tablets of the Ten Commandments
- A jar of manna—the food that had appeared in the desert
- And, later, Aaron's rod, which had miraculously sprouted flowers

So what was the Ark, exactly? A chest? A holy safe? A divine weapon? The answer seems to be: all of the above.

The Ark didn't just sit in a temple. It moved.

According to ancient texts, the Ark led the Israelites through the desert for 40 years. It was carried at the front of their line. When the Ark moved, so did the people. When it stopped, they stopped.

And weird things happened around it.

In one story, the Ark was carried into battle against the city of Jericho. The priests marched around the walls for seven days, blowing trumpets—and the walls fell.

In another, a man touched the Ark to steady it when it wobbled—and dropped dead instantly.

Even enemies feared it. The Philistines captured the Ark once and brought it into their temple. Within days, their idol statue had toppled over, their people got sick, and the Ark was quickly returned.

It wasn't just an object.
It was treated like a presence.

And Then It Was Gone

Eventually, King Solomon built a temple in Jerusalem—a permanent home for the Ark. It was placed in the Holy of

Holies, the most sacred room, entered only once a year by the high priest.

And then... silence.

Sometime during the Babylonian invasion of Jerusalem (around 586 BCE), the Ark vanished. The Temple was destroyed. The city was taken. But there's no record of the Ark being captured—or saved.

Did the priests hide it in a cave? Did it get smuggled out of the city? Or was it taken... somewhere else?

Clues are scattered, but inconclusive.

- One ancient text says the prophet Jeremiah hid it in a mountain.
- Some believe it lies beneath the Temple Mount, where digging is restricted.
- Others point to Ethiopia, where monks at a remote church claim to guard the Ark to this day—though no one's allowed to see it.

What Was It, Really?

Some say the Ark was just a box—important, yes, but not supernatural. Others believe it may have had real physical properties: perhaps electricity, strange acoustics, or even ancient technology that's been lost.

But maybe its real power wasn't what was inside... Maybe it was the fear, awe, and mystery people placed around it.

Even today, the Ark appears in books, documentaries, and movies—not as treasure, but as a puzzle waiting to be solved.

A perfectly described object. A trail of clues. And a disappearance that has never been explained.

The last place it was seen was behind the veil of a temple.

Now it's behind the veil of time.

Let's keep looking.

JOAN OF ARC

How did a young girl from a small village become one of the most famous figures in history?

What were the mysterious visions and voices she claimed to hear?

She couldn't read. She couldn't write. She was a peasant girl from a village so small it barely had a name.

And yet, at age thirteen, Joan of Arc began hearing voices—loud, clear, and impossible to ignore. They told her France was in danger. They told her she had a mission. They told her to lead an army.

And somehow... she did.

She convinced generals. She met with kings. She marched into battle wearing armor, waving a banner. She didn't flinch under fire. She never learned to fight—but her side kept winning.

So who was she listening to?

Joan said the voices came from saints. But not everyone believed her. Some thought she was chosen. Others thought she was dangerous. A few thought she was lying. Even today, no one can explain what she heard—or why she followed it so completely.

Was she a prophet? A soldier? A girl caught in the middle of history?

There are letters. Records. Trial transcripts. But some questions still whisper through the centuries.

Let's gather the evidence, replay the voices, and figure out what really guided the girl who would not back down.

When Joan was born in 1412, France was losing a long, brutal war against England. The French crown was divided. The English controlled huge parts of the country. Everyone was tired. Beaten. Afraid.

And then a teenage girl walked into the royal court and said, "I have a message from God."

She didn't look powerful. She wore rough clothes. She had no title, no training. But she spoke with fire. She told the Dauphin—the prince waiting to become king—that she would see him crowned at Reims, the traditional site of French coronations.

People laughed. Then stared. Then listened.

And somehow... she was right.

Joan never swung a sword in combat, but she changed the energy of the battlefield. She rode at the front. She raised morale. She turned hopeless troops into believers. She carried a white banner with Jesus and angels painted on it. She claimed it had been shown to her in a vision.

In 1429, she helped lift the siege of Orléans, a battle France wasn't supposed to win. Weeks later, the Dauphin was crowned King Charles VII—exactly as Joan had predicted.

For a moment, the war seemed to turn. So did history.

But the voices didn't stop. They grew louder. More demanding.

And Joan's story was far from over.

In 1430, Joan was captured near Compiègne and handed over to the English. She was put on trial—not for her military actions, but for heresy: claiming to hear voices from God.

She faced over a dozen judges. No lawyer. Just questions.

Were the voices real? "They never failed me," she said. Were they from God? "I believe they were," she answered.

She didn't break. But they found another way to trap her.

While in prison, Joan wore men's clothing—armor, trousers, tunics. She said it helped her avoid assault and gave her freedom to move. But the court called it sinful.

She was told to stop. When she put the clothes back on, they said she had relapsed. That was enough.

She was found guilty.

On May 30, 1431, Joan of Arc was burned at the stake in Rouen's town square. She was nineteen.

Witnesses said she called out to Jesus as the flames rose.

Twenty-five years later, the Church reexamined her trial. It was declared invalid. She was cleared of all charges.

In 1920, she was named a saint.

That's the mystery.

Was she mentally ill? Maybe—but her answers never changed.

Was she lying? Then how did she change the course of a war?

Or… was she actually chosen?

She predicted victories. She crowned a king. She followed her voices to the very end.

The clues are here. The records are real.

What she heard—we still can't explain.

NAZCA LINES

How did ancient people create such huge, precise designs without modern tools?

Why did they make them so large that they're only visible from the sky?

You're walking through the desert. Flat. Empty. Silent.

Then someone shows you a photograph from above—and your jaw drops.

You weren't walking through nothing.

You were walking across a hummingbird.

Or a monkey. Or a giant spider.
Perfectly carved into the Earth.

But here's the twist: You can't see the full design from the ground. You'd have to be hundreds of feet in the air.

So who made them? And how?

The answers are... Sketchy.

The Nazca Lines stretch across the dry coastal plains of southern Peru. Hundreds of them. Some are simple shapes. Others form spirals, zigzags, and massive animal figures— each hundreds of feet across.

They were first spotted by airplane pilots in the 1920s, but locals had known about them for centuries. The oldest ones were made more than 2,000 years ago.

There's no paint. No tools. Just grooves cut into the sun-baked ground, revealing lighter-colored earth below. The dryness of the desert helped preserve them.

But the real mystery?
Why would anyone go to such lengths to draw something so massive—that they could never see in full?

Scientists agree the Nazca people built the lines between 500 BCE and 500 CE. But what the lines mean is still up for debate.

Some researchers think they were part of religious ceremonies—paths that were walked during rituals.

Others believe they point to underground water sources or even map the stars.

A few lines line up with solstices and mountain peaks. Some seem purely artistic. Others feel too deliberate to be random.

And then there are the more extreme theories: alien messages, ancient astronauts, landing strips for flying machines.

Most scientists say those aren't likely. But the lines themselves? Still unsolved.

That part is surprisingly simple. A team of people could use stakes, ropes, and basic tools to mark out the lines. Once planned, they would scrape away the dark topsoil to reveal the pale clay beneath.

In 2019, researchers using drones discovered even more figures—including some so faded they'd never been seen before.

Whoever made these shapes didn't just want to be seen.

They wanted to be remembered.

The Nazca Lines aren't just art. They're messages written into the earth—and no one knows what they say.

Were they prayers? Maps? A giant calendar?
Or something else we've yet to understand?

What we do know:
- They were carefully made.
- They were meant to last.
- And they were built by people who never saw their own designs.

All we can do now is study the shapes, follow the tracks, and see what the desert can still tell us after all these years.

ROANOKE ISLAND

CROATOAN

What happened to the people of Roanoke Colony after they vanished?

Why were the strange words "Croatoan" and "CRO" carved into trees?

They found a single word carved into a tree.

No bodies. No graves. No signs of struggle. Just that one word—CROATOAN—etched into the wood like a message, or maybe a warning.

It was 1590. The English supply ship had finally returned, three years late. Captain John White, the appointed governor of the colony, stepped ashore and stared in disbelief.

The settlement was gone.

No smoke. No voices. No footprints in the dirt. Just weathered walls, dismantled cabins, and silence where over 100 men, women, and children had once lived.

Let's follow the clues.

Clue #1: the missing colonists.

In 1587, England had sent 115 settlers to establish a new colony on Roanoke Island, just off the coast of present-day North Carolina. It was meant to be the first permanent English settlement in the New World. Among them was White's own daughter, Eleanor Dare, and his infant granddaughter—Virginia Dare, the first English child born in America.

Soon after their arrival, White returned to England for supplies, promising to return swiftly. But war with Spain delayed him. By the time he came back, the colony had vanished.

Clue #2: no signs of violence.

White and his men found the fort's perimeter neatly dismantled—not destroyed. Belongings were gone, not scattered. The palisade had been taken down with care. This didn't look like a massacre or a raid.

It looked like a retreat.

Clue #3: the carvings.

The only physical evidence left behind were two carvings. One on a post: CRO, and another, deeper into the woods:

CROATOAN. That was the name of a nearby island, home to a Native American tribe friendly to the English.

Before he left, White had told the colonists that if they had to move, they should carve a message—and if they were in danger, they should carve a cross. There was no cross.

Just that word: CROATOAN.

Clue #4: no rescue.

White wanted to sail to Croatoan immediately. But a storm hit. His ship was damaged, his crew refused to go farther, and they turned back to England.

He never saw the colonists again.

Clue #5: strange reports.

Years passed. Other English colonists tried to settle the region. Some said they saw children with gray eyes and European features living among local tribes. Others claimed to hear rumors of settlers absorbed into native communities—marrying, adapting, surviving.

In 1607, Captain John Smith of Jamestown heard from the Powhatan people that a nearby tribe had wiped out a group of white settlers living inland. He believed it could have been the Roanoke colonists. But again, there were no remains. No proof.

Clue #6: the Dare Stones.

Starting in 1937, a series of engraved stones were discovered across the American South. The first one was allegedly written by Eleanor Dare. It told of suffering, disease, and death. Later stones described a journey inland and marked graves.

Some believed they were authentic relics. Others called them hoaxes—manufactured to stir up excitement. Most historians dismiss them. But a few still argue that at least one might be real.

Clue #7: archaeology.

Modern digs have uncovered European artifacts on Croatoan Island—now called Hatteras Island—including a sword hilt, a slate writing tablet, and copper rings. But none are definitive proof that Roanoke's settlers moved there. They could've belonged to traders, castaways, or other visitors.

Other digs near the Chowan River have found 16th-century English pottery and weapons, suggesting some survivors may have moved inland. But again—no names, no graves, no clear line to Roanoke.

Clue #8: the DNA hunt.

Today, researchers are turning to genetic clues. The Lost Colony DNA Project has collected DNA samples from local families with oral traditions of English ancestry predating Jamestown. The goal: to find genetic links to the vanished colonists.

So far, no breakthrough. But the search continues.

What happened to the Lost Colony?

Some believe they starved, or were killed by hostile tribes. Others think they moved to Croatoan or joined nearby villages to survive. A few believe the settlers split up, some going north, some inland, some lost to time.

No bones. No documents. Just stories.

And one carved word. It's not enough. But it might be a trailhead.

Maybe the answer lies buried in sand, or passed down in blood. Maybe it's hidden in a forgotten trunk, or a lost scrap of parchment. Maybe it was never meant to be found at all.

Some mysteries rot. Others vanish.

The mystery of Roanoke?

It still waits.

THE
DANCING
PLAGUE
OF 1518

What caused hundreds of people to
dance without stopping in the streets?

How did this strange frenzy spread
to so many others?

It started with one woman.

On a summer day in 1518, in the town of Strasbourg, Frau Troffea stepped into the street... and began to dance. No music. No audience. No explanation. Just swaying, twirling, moving.

She danced for hours. Then days.

Then others joined her.

Within a week, dozens of people were dancing in the streets. By the end of the month, hundreds were caught in the same strange trance—unable to stop.

Not for food. Not for rest. Not even for sleep.

Some collapsed. Some broke bones. Some reportedly danced themselves to death.

The town had no idea what was happening. And five hundred years later, we still don't.

So what was the Dancing Plague?

This really happened. It's not legend, not folklore, not a twisted fairy tale.

Multiple written sources from the time confirm the outbreak. City officials recorded it. Doctors observed it. Priests wrote about it in horror. In one account, a man danced for six days straight before collapsing.

And it wasn't joyful. The dancing was described as painful, frantic, and terrifying.

Some dancers screamed for help even as their bodies kept moving. Others bled from their feet. Eyewitnesses said it looked like possession.

But if it wasn't a party... what was it?

The city turned to doctors. Their diagnosis? "Hot blood."

The cure? More dancing.

Yes—really. Officials believed the dancers had to "sweat out" whatever caused the affliction. They even hired musicians and cleared space in the town square to give the dancers more room.

But the problem didn't go away.

It spread.

Eventually, the city shut down the music, banned dancing, and ordered dancers to be taken away—some to shrines, some to isolation. Only then did the outbreak fade.

But the questions didn't.

Theory #1: Mass Hysteria

One of the most common theories is what we now call mass psychogenic illness—a kind of shared mental and physical reaction to extreme stress.

In the 1500s, life was brutal. Strasbourg had recently suffered floods, famines, and disease. Some historians think the townspeople were already stretched to their limit—and that stress triggered a strange psychological reaction that spread person to person.

This kind of group behavior has happened before: laughing fits in schools, fainting spells in crowds, even itching outbreaks with no physical cause.

So maybe the Dancing Plague was a real illness... with no virus. No bacteria. Just fear, tension, and something deep inside the brain snapping.

But if that's true, why dancing?

Theory #2: Toxic Bread

Another theory points to something physical: ergot.

Ergot is a fungus that grows on rye in wet conditions. If you eat it, it can cause hallucinations, spasms, and convulsions. It's chemically related to LSD. Some historians think a batch of contaminated grain could have triggered the outbreak.

It sounds possible—until you ask a few more questions.

If it was ergot poisoning, why didn't the symptoms hit all at once? Why did it last for weeks? And why did the "dancing" spread by observation, not by eating?

Ergot can make people twitch and shake. But dance for days? That part's harder to explain.

Theory #3: Something Else Entirely

There are other ideas, too.

Some blame religious panic—fear of sin or judgment. Others suggest secret rituals, group hypnosis, or unknown neurological conditions. Some believe it was all exaggerated by rumor. And a few historians admit something simple:

We don't know.

Because nothing quite like it has happened since—not at this scale, not this dramatically.

The Dancing Plague remains one of the strangest unsolved outbreaks in recorded history.

We have written records. Names. Locations. Death tolls. But no cause.

Was it fear? Fungus? Famine? Faith?

Or was it something that doesn't fit in any medical book?

What's clear is this: in 1518, a town watched its people move until they fell—and nobody could stop it.

THE OAK ISLAND MONEY PIT

What treasure lies hidden beneath
the surface of Oak Island?

Who built the tricky traps and
tunnels that keep treasure hunters
away?

They found the first clue under an old oak tree.

It was 1795. Three teenage boys on Oak Island, just off the coast of Nova Scotia, noticed a strange dip in the ground. A pulley hung from a branch above it—too old to be in use, too suspicious to ignore. So they started digging.

At ten feet, they hit a layer of logs.

At twenty feet, another.

Every ten feet, more wood, like someone had built a staircase deep into the earth.

Something was down there. Something hidden.

They had no idea they'd just opened one of the most expensive, dangerous, and frustrating treasure hunts in history.

More than two centuries later, no one has reached the bottom.

And no one has figured out who built it, what's inside it, or why it fights back.

A Hole with a Mind of Its Own

The deeper people dug, the stranger it got.

In the 1800s, workers found stone tools that didn't belong. Coconut fibers—impossible to find naturally that far north. A flat tablet carved with symbols, rumored to say: "Forty feet below, two million pounds are buried."

Then, suddenly, the pit flooded with seawater. No storm. No warning. Just—water. Lots of it.

They tried to drain it. It refilled.

They dug new shafts nearby. Those flooded too.

It was as if someone had built a machine—a trap—to protect whatever lay below.

And it was working.

Engineers eventually discovered that the pit is connected to flood tunnels—manmade channels linking the shaft to the sea.

Some believe they were lined with clay and filled with smooth stones to act like underwater tripwires. Dig too far, and the tunnels activate, flooding everything.

One pit collapsed and pulled tools down with it. Another created suction, like the island was breathing.

No matter how close treasure hunters came, the pit stayed one step ahead.

So what's buried down there?

That's the million-dollar question.

Some say pirate treasure—maybe Captain Kidd or Blackbeard. Others say it's royal gold, hidden during the French Revolution. Some believe it holds secret scrolls or artifacts buried by the Knights Templar.

There are hints of something.

Broken bits of parchment.

Traces of gold on drill bits.

Chains. Buttons. Wood from centuries-old ships.

Even rumors of Roman swords and mysterious metal crosses.

But still—no treasure chest. No vault. No grand reveal.

And the deeper the dig, the more complicated it becomes.

Over 200 years, dozens of excavation teams have spent millions of dollars trying to crack the pit's secrets. Some have died. Others gave up. A few think it was all a hoax—an elaborate prank built to fool greedy treasure hunters.

But if it was a hoax...

Who would go through the trouble of digging booby-trapped tunnels, carving coded stones, and engineering a flooding mechanism that still works after 200 years?

Even skeptics admit that someone went to a lot of trouble to keep people out.

And they've done a good job.

Today, Oak Island is still being searched. Modern teams use sonar scans, drilling rigs, underwater cameras, and high-tech excavation gear. They've mapped out side tunnels, detected hidden chambers, and even sent probes deeper than ever before.

But the truth remains buried.

No name. No plans. No clear explanation.

Just a hole in the ground that refuses to give up its story.

So what is the Oak Island Money Pit?

A buried treasure?

A decoy?

Or a warning never meant to be uncovered?

The mystery remains unsolved, waiting for the next explorer to study shaft diagrams, trace the flooding traps. and see if this centuries-old mystery was ever meant to be solved.

THE
BERMUDA
TRIANGLE

Why do ships and planes disappear in the Bermuda Triangle?

What causes strange compass readings and navigational problems?

There's no sign in the sky when you enter it. No sudden storm. No ripple in the water.

Just open sea—blue, calm, and wide.

But somewhere between Miami, Bermuda, and Puerto Rico, things start to vanish.

Boats. Planes. Whole crews.

And the strange part? They often disappear without a trace.

No mayday calls. No wreckage. No explanation.

That's what turned this patch of ocean into a legend.

But is the Bermuda Triangle really dangerous?

Let's follow the clues.

One of the first major incidents happened in 1945. Five U.S. Navy planes—Flight 19—were on a routine training run when their leader radioed that they were lost. The sky looked "weird," his compass was spinning, and he couldn't tell east from west. The entire squadron disappeared. A rescue plane sent to find them also vanished.

Six planes. Twenty-seven men. No wreckage found.

That was clue #1.

Reporters gave the area a name: the Bermuda Triangle.

Soon, other stories came to light.

The USS Cyclops, a Navy supply ship with over 300 people onboard, disappeared in 1918. No distress signal. No debris. A massive search turned up nothing.

In 1963, the SS Marine Sulphur Queen vanished with 39 men aboard. It had been carrying molten sulfur in a converted World War II tanker. Not a single lifeboat was recovered.

More cases followed: yachts found adrift with meals still on the table. Planes gone off radar. Entire crews missing from ships, no sign of struggle.

That's when the theories started.

Some blamed magnetic anomalies—natural glitches in the Earth's magnetic field that could confuse compasses or instruments. Others suggested rogue waves, sudden and violent walls of water that could capsize ships in seconds. A few pointed to methane gas eruptions from the seafloor, which might reduce water density and cause ships to sink without warning.

But even those don't explain everything.

Why no debris? Why no signals?

Why do so many cases involve experienced crews, good weather, and calm seas?

Some researchers believe the mystery is exaggerated. When you compare the Bermuda Triangle to other busy shipping areas, the number of incidents isn't much higher. They say it's not a mystery—it's just math, weather, and bad luck.

But others aren't convinced.

Flight 19's radio logs, for example, are full of contradictions. Some planes lost contact early, while others were still heard for hours. Navy reports later blamed "pilot error," but even that didn't explain how trained fliers could vanish without leaving a trace.

The ocean floor in the area is also unusually deep—some spots drop over five miles straight down. A sunken plane or ship could simply vanish beneath layers of sand, out of reach of searchers.

So what's the truth?

Natural forces? Navigation mistakes? Or something we still don't understand?

The Bermuda Triangle has no official boundaries. It's not marked on maps. But the stories—documented, puzzling, and often unsolved—are real.

And they leave behind the most haunting clue of all:

An empty silence where something should be.

The case isn't closed.

And the sea is still watching.

VOYNICH
MANUSCRIPT

What language or code is hidden in
the pages of the Voynich Manuscript,
and can it ever be understood?

Who was behind this mysterious
book, and what purpose did it serve?

It has pages made of calfskin. Ink that's faded but not smudged. Bright illustrations of plants no one recognizes. Diagrams of moons and stars that don't match any known system. And a script—an entire written language—that no one has ever seen anywhere else in the world.

That's the Voynich Manuscript.

Found in a locked chest in 1912 by a rare book dealer named Wilfrid Voynich, the book appeared to be very old—and very weird. It was about the size of a modern textbook, full of drawings and diagrams. But the text? It didn't match Latin, Greek, Arabic, Hebrew, or anything else.

It wasn't just a code. It was a full writing system that didn't appear to come from anywhere.

The pages were filled with looping letters and made-up words that repeated like real sentences. But after more than a century of study, no one has ever cracked it.

What is the Voynich Manuscript? A hoax? A lost language? A secret code? A forgotten science?

Every theory brings new questions. Every clue leads deeper into the mystery.

The book is divided into sections. Some show plants—detailed roots, stems, blossoms. Some almost look real. Others are pure fantasy. Botanists haven't been able to match a single one.

Other pages show strange diagrams of women floating in green liquid, surrounded by stars and pipes. Some pages look like star charts. Others look like anatomy textbooks—if humans had moons orbiting their heads and bathed in plumbing systems.

Still, the text rolls on, sentence after sentence in a language that no one else has ever written or read. Entire pages are filled with it. There are no punctuation marks. No titles. Just a smooth, continuous flow of alien-looking letters.

Experts tried everything.

In the 1940s, World War II codebreakers studied the book. These were the same people who cracked Nazi codes. The Voynich? No luck.

In the 2000s, artificial intelligence programs scanned the text for patterns. The results were strange. The writing followed the rules of real languages—like grammar, repetition, and structure—but didn't match any known one.

In 2019, a researcher claimed the book was written in scrambled Hebrew. It made headlines but was quickly challenged by other scholars. Others said it was shorthand Latin, or a made-up language written by someone in a trance.

Some believe it was all a trick—a fake book written to fool rich collectors. But that theory has problems. The patterns are too consistent. The fake language is too natural. Faking this— page after page—would have taken years.

And the biggest twist? The pages are real.

In 2009, radiocarbon testing dated the manuscript's calfskin vellum to between 1404 and 1438. That means the book is over 600 years old.

The ink is from the same period. It's not a modern fake.

Who wrote it? No one knows.

It may have passed through the hands of Emperor Rudolf II in the 1600s. He thought it might be the work of Roger Bacon, a scientist from the 1200s. That theory has faded, but others remain.

Some think it came from a secret society. Others believe it was a private research notebook, encoded to keep its knowledge hidden.

But if it was science, why include plants that don't exist? Why use a language no one else could read? Why make a book so careful, so detailed, and then bury its meaning completely?

The Voynich Manuscript seems designed to be understood—and impossible to translate.

The illustrations are clear and deliberate. The text is smooth and flowing. It doesn't look random. It looks like someone was trying to explain something that made total sense to them—and absolutely no one else.

Some think it's a lost civilization's last words. Others think it's just nonsense dressed up to look meaningful.

But the book never breaks character.

It remains steady, silent, strange.

No other copy has ever been found. No similar language. No follow-up volume.

All we have is one book, 240 pages, and a message no one can read.

Not a single sentence. Not a single word.

The Voynich Manuscript might be the most unreadable book in the world—and that's exactly what makes it unforgettable.

Let's turn the pages, follow the patterns, and see if this ancient voice is finally ready to speak.

THE LOCH NESS MONSTER

Does the Loch Ness Monster really
live in the depths of Scotland's
mysterious lake?

Could Nessie be a creature from
ancient times, or is she simply a
legend that's grown over time?

The water is dark, nearly black.

Loch Ness is over 20 miles long, 700 feet deep in places, and surrounded by misty hills and pine trees. On calm days, it's like glass. On stormy days, it churns like the ocean.

And for nearly 1,500 years, people have reported something moving beneath its surface.

They say it's large. Serpentine. Sometimes with a long neck. Sometimes with humps. Always fast—and always gone before anyone gets too close.

It's been called a kelpie, a dragon, a sea serpent.

Today, we call it the Loch Ness Monster.

And no matter how many scientists roll their eyes, the sightings haven't stopped.

So what's swimming in Loch Ness?

A hoax? A misidentified animal?

Or a living mystery that's been hiding in plain sight?

The earliest report comes from the year 565. A saint named Columba wrote that a giant water beast attacked one of his followers swimming across the loch. He prayed. The monster vanished. The story was written down. And that was the first clue.

Then, silence—for more than a thousand years.

But in the 1930s, something changed.

A new road was built along the shoreline. More people had cars. Suddenly, there were more eyes on the water.

In April 1933, a couple driving past the loch said they saw a creature crossing the road to the water. It was huge, they said, with a long neck. Their report made the newspaper. From that point on, the legend exploded.

Sightings poured in. Tourists arrived with cameras. Fishermen swore they'd seen it. Boaters said something large swam under them, casting massive shadows.

Then came the photo.

In 1934, a doctor named Robert Kenneth Wilson submitted a photograph to the Daily Mail. It showed something in the water—just a head and neck, rising out of the loch. The image was grainy and shadowy, but the shape was unforgettable.

It became known as "The Surgeon's Photo," and it's one of the most famous cryptid images in history.

For decades, it was considered the best proof of Nessie's existence.

Then, in 1994, a new story surfaced: it was a hoax. A model. A toy submarine with a fake head glued on.

That revelation shook the believers—but it didn't stop the sightings.

Because not all evidence comes in photos.

Sonar scans have picked up large moving objects beneath the surface. Divers have reported strange shapes in the murky depths. Drone footage has shown ripples without a clear cause. And over the years, more than 1,000 people have signed written eyewitness accounts.

Some of them are tourists. Some are lifelong locals. Some are scientists.

So what are they seeing?

Some theories are simple: waves caused by boat wakes. Logs. Swimming deer. Eels. Otters. Birds diving at strange angles. In the right light, even a floating branch can look like a sea serpent.

Other theories go bigger: a hidden population of giant eels. A new species of freshwater seal. Or even a surviving plesiosaur, a marine reptile thought to have gone extinct with the dinosaurs.

But the plesiosaur idea has problems. Loch Ness was under ice during the last Ice Age. It's not connected to the ocean. And the water is cold, dark, and low in nutrients—probably not enough to support a family of prehistoric monsters.

Still, the shape that people describe—small head, long neck, humped back—keeps coming up.

One sighting in 1951 described a creature crossing the road again. In 1960, an aeronautical engineer filmed something moving in the water at high speed. In 2011, sonar picked up a 60-foot object moving deep beneath a boat. In 2020, satellite images showed a long shape in the loch near the surface.

None of it is solid proof.

But none of it has been completely explained either.

And that's what keeps people coming back.

Today, Loch Ness is one of the most studied bodies of water in the world. Boats with sonar patrol it year-round. Drones scan it from above. Divers explore the caves and silt beds. Scientists have taken environmental DNA samples to test for unusual species. So far, they've found nothing extraordinary.

But the loch is big. The water is dark. And the mystery is deep.

So what is the Loch Ness Monster? The creature may be silent. But the clues are still there—slippery, shadowy, and just out of reach.

So keep scanning the surface, searching the sonar, and see if this ancient shape ever comes into focus.

THE MAN IN THE IRON MASK

Who was the Man in the Iron Mask, really?

Why was his identity such a well-kept secret?

e never gave his name. His face was never seen. For over thirty years, he was locked away in prison after prison—always in silence, always in disguise.

And in death, his identity vanished with him.

Who was the Man in the Iron Mask?

Let's examine the evidence.

The story begins in France, in the late 1600s, during the reign of King Louis XIV. A mysterious prisoner was transferred to the Bastille, the famous fortress-prison in Paris. His guards were given strict orders: no one was to see his face. He wore a mask at all times—possibly made of black velvet, but later rumored to be iron. Even his name was erased. Records simply called him "the unknown prisoner."

But this wasn't an ordinary criminal.

He was treated unusually well. His cell was clean. He had fine food. He read books and played the lute. His jailers respected him—and followed strict rules of secrecy. One even carried a loaded pistol with orders to kill the man if he ever spoke his name.

So who needed to be hidden so completely?

Clue #1: His arrest and imprisonment were overseen by Louis XIV's powerful minister, the Marquis de Louvois. Only the king's inner circle knew the truth.

Clue #2: The prisoner was moved frequently, from one high-security fortress to another, always under the same warden—Bénigne Dauvergne de Saint-Mars. His movements were tracked with precision. He was no random detainee.

In 1703, the masked man died in the Bastille. He was buried under a false name: "Marchioly." His cell was scrubbed, his belongings burned, and his story buried with him.

But not for long.

Writers and historians began piecing together clues. In the 1800s, Alexandre Dumas turned the mystery into legend in *The Vicomte de Bragelonne*, suggesting the man was the king's secret twin brother—locked away to protect the crown.

It made for great fiction. But was it true?

Some theories suggest he was a disgraced general or court official who knew too much. Others say he was an Italian nobleman who offended the king. One popular guess? That he was Louis XIV's older brother—or even his father's illegitimate son.

What we know for sure is this:

The French government went to extreme lengths to hide his identity.

And that raises the most important question of all:

What did he know—or *who* was he—that made him dangerous enough to disappear behind a mask for life?

The Man in the Iron Mask never spoke his name.

And no one has spoken it since.

THE GHOST SHIP
OCTAVIUS

What happened to the crew of the
Octavius that left them frozen in
time?

Was it the frigid cold, starvation, or
maybe a mysterious illness?

I t wasn't on any map.

No distress signal. No call for help.

Just a wooden hull drifting silently off the coast of Greenland, sails torn, deck covered in ice. When the crew of the whaling ship *Herald* spotted it in 1775, they knew something was wrong. The vessel didn't respond. It didn't steer. It just drifted, lifeless in the current.

So they boarded her.

The ship's name was painted in faded letters across the stern: *Octavius*.

What the boarding party found would become one of the most chilling maritime legends ever recorded.

Let's follow the clues.

Below deck, everything looked frozen in time. Tables still set. Cargo still in place. Not a sign of struggle or panic. Just cold, silent stillness.

And in the captain's cabin—was the captain himself.

Still at his desk. Dead. Frozen stiff. Pen still in hand. Beside him was the ship's logbook, brittle with frost. Crew members—also frozen—lay in their hammocks or crumpled in corners. No sign of injury. No violence. Just a ship full of bodies, preserved by cold and time.

The crew of the *Herald* took only part of the log, unsure whether to believe what they were reading. Then they left the *Octavius* to the sea.

It was never seen again.

The partial log told a strange story. The *Octavius* had departed England in 1761, bound for China. She arrived safely, delivered her cargo, and then, according to the log, made a bold decision: rather than return the long way around

Africa, the captain chose to attempt the Northwest Passage—an unproven, ice-filled route over the top of North America.

If the logs were accurate, the *Octavius* had been lost at sea for over 13 years.

Here's where things get weirder.

When the *Herald* found the *Octavius* off Greenland, it was west of where the ship had supposedly tried to pass through the Arctic. If the story's true, that means the *Octavius* completed the Northwest Passage—but too late for anyone to know.

And no one survived to report it.

So what happened?

Let's look at the knowns.

First: the Northwest Passage in the 1760s was a death trap. Ships were crushed by shifting sea ice. Crews froze, starved, or vanished into the white.

Second: the Arctic can preserve a body for decades. Cold, dry air and isolation make for perfect natural mummification. The idea of a frozen crew isn't impossible.

Third: the story never appeared in British naval logs. The name *Octavius* doesn't match any official records. No departure manifests. No mention in trade routes or government archives. That's a big red flag.

Could it be a ghost story, made up by sailors and passed around docks for generations?

Possibly. But it has strange consistency.

The story first appeared in maritime lore in the early 19th century—decades before Victorian ghost tales were common. And unlike most tall tales, it doesn't rely on curses, sea monsters, or haunted storms. Just cold facts: an abandoned ship, a dead crew, a pen frozen in the hand of a long-dead captain.

That's what makes it stick.

Some theorists believe the ship was real, but the name was changed or misremembered. Others think the *Octavius* was a composite—a mix of real sightings and borrowed details from other shipwrecks. Ghost ship sightings weren't rare in the 1700s and 1800s. In a world of long voyages and limited communication, anything abandoned at sea sparked imagination.

Still, if it's fiction, it's a clever one.

The *Octavius* wasn't described as cursed. There was no evil to fight. Just a captain who rolled the dice on a deadly route and lost. His crew, wrapped in wool and frost, became silent witnesses to a journey no one had made before.

If it happened, it was the first ship to complete the Northwest Passage.

But no one got to celebrate.

The sea doesn't always roar. Sometimes it whispers. It freezes. It forgets.

And sometimes, it gives back a ghost.

The final entry in the *Octavius* logbook ends mid-sentence.

As if the hand that wrote it simply stopped.

As if, in that moment, time did too.

THE
ANTIKYTHERA
MECHANISM

How did ancient Greeks make something so advanced without modern technology?

What exactly was its purpose?

I t started with a shipwreck.

In 1900, a group of sponge divers were exploring the waters off the Greek island of Antikythera when a storm forced them to take shelter. While diving for sponges, one of them surfaced in a panic—he said he'd seen dead bodies in armor.

What they found instead was a Roman-era shipwreck, over 2,000 years old, scattered across the seafloor. Inside: marble statues, bronze arms, glassware, and ancient coins. But among the treasure, something strange surfaced—a lump of corroded bronze and rotting wood.

No one paid it much attention.

Not at first.

But years later, that lump broke apart in storage, revealing something impossible: bronze gears. Cogs. Inscribed markings in ancient Greek. It looked like the shattered remains of a machine.

And it didn't belong to that time.

Let's follow the clues.

The object came to be known as the Antikythera Mechanism. At first glance, it looked like a badly rusted clock—except it was made in the first or second century BCE. That's over 1,000 years before the first mechanical clocks appeared in Europe.

The mystery deepened.

In the 1950s, British science historian Derek de Solla Price began studying the device using X-rays. What he discovered stunned him: this wasn't just a simple tool. It was a complex gear-driven machine, likely used to model the motions of the heavens.

Over 30 bronze gears, layered and connected, turning with astonishing precision.

But what did it do?

And who built it?

As more imaging techniques were developed, the fog began to lift. The mechanism wasn't random. It had clear functions. It tracked the positions of the sun and moon. It predicted eclipses. It showed the phases of the moon. Some believe it even tracked the motions of planets.

It could also calculate future dates on multiple ancient calendars—Greek, Egyptian, and Babylonian.

All packed into a box the size of a shoebox.

The level of detail was jaw-dropping. The mechanism included a spiral dial to track a 223-month lunar cycle. Another dial predicted solar eclipses, even warning of those linked to bad omens. It modeled the elliptical orbit of the moon, using a pin-and-slot mechanism to mimic its speeding up and slowing down—centuries before Kepler and Newton described elliptical motion with math.

Clue after clue, one message became clear:

This was not some crude prototype.

This was advanced.

So how could ancient Greeks—who worked with hand tools, who didn't have precision metal lathes or industrial machines—build something so intricate?

And why was it lost?

The shipwreck was dated to around 60 BCE, but the mechanism itself may be older—possibly made between 150 and 100 BCE. That places it in the same era as Archimedes and Hipparchus, a time when Greek astronomers were making bold strides in understanding the cosmos.

Some researchers believe the mechanism came from Rhodes, a hub of ancient science and home to famous astronomers. Others connect it to the library of Pergamon or a lost workshop in Corinth.

But no other mechanism like it has ever been found.

Not even close. That's what makes it so strange.

If the Greeks had the knowledge to build this machine, why wasn't it mentioned in more texts? Why wasn't it copied, refined, and spread? Did the secret vanish in the fires of Rome, or in the silence that followed the fall of ancient science?

We may never know.

Even today, researchers are still decoding the inscriptions. Some fragments are tiny—smaller than a postage stamp. Others hint at functions we still don't fully understand. Modern reconstructions based on scans and fragments suggest it was once housed in a wooden case with a front and back dial. The user would turn a crank to simulate celestial time.

A hand-cranked analog computer, built 2,000 years ago.

The Antikythera Mechanism didn't just measure time. It modeled the universe as the Greeks understood it—ordered, mechanical, beautiful.

But it wasn't built to be seen. It wasn't a statue or a temple. It was a tool. A machine. Possibly for teaching. Possibly for navigation. Possibly for ritual or prediction.

And maybe that's why it was forgotten.

The ship that carried it sank. The minds that built it faded.

And the machine itself lay buried underwater for 2,000 years—until a storm, a curious diver, and a broken piece of bronze gave the world its most mysterious computer.

The mechanism still isn't fully understood. But one thing is clear: The ancient world was smarter, stranger, and more advanced than we ever imagined. And this wasn't their peak.

It was only what they left behind.

SECRET SIDE QUEST UNLOCKED!

Enjoying the journey so far?
Want to help fellow explorers
crack these mysteries too?

Just scan the code and leave a quick
review—it's like leaving a clue on
the map for the next brave
adventurer.

*Even one sentence
helps more than
you know.*

THE SHROUD OF TURIN

Could this mysterious cloth
actually show the face of Jesus Christ?

How could an image like this be
made over 600 years ago without
modern technology?

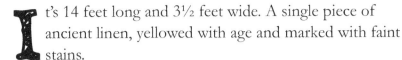

I t's 14 feet long and 3½ feet wide. A single piece of ancient linen, yellowed with age and marked with faint stains.

But step back.

There's a face.

A body.

Front and back. Arms folded. Feet crossed. Wounds at the wrists. A crown of what looks like thorns. Blood running down. The image is pale and ghostly—like a negative photo burned into cloth.

It's called the Shroud of Turin.

And some believe it is the burial cloth of Jesus Christ.

Others believe it's the most convincing forgery in history.

Let's follow the clues.

The shroud first appears in the historical record in the 1350s, in a small church in Lirey, France. No one knows exactly where it came from. The local bishop was suspicious and declared it a fake. But that didn't stop pilgrims from coming. Or the rumors from spreading.

By the 1500s, the cloth had been moved to Turin, Italy. It was stored in a royal chapel, shown to crowds on special occasions. When a fire threatened it in 1532, it was saved—though scorch marks and water stains remain. Eventually, it came under the protection of the Vatican.

Then came photography.

In 1898, an Italian named Secondo Pia took the first official photograph of the shroud. When he developed the negative, he was shocked. The figure on the cloth appeared with stunning clarity—more lifelike in the photo than on the cloth itself. It was as if the image had been created *as* a photographic negative... centuries before photography existed.

That was clue #1.

The world took notice.

Researchers began to study the cloth—examining the weave of the linen, the blood patterns, and the body proportions. Some claimed the wounds matched the crucifixion described in the Gospels: nail marks in the wrists (not the palms, as often shown in art), a spear wound in the side, and bleeding across the scalp.

Others noted strange details.

There was no outline, no pigment. The image appeared to be a change in the chemical structure of the fibers themselves—not paint, not ink. It couldn't be scrubbed off, because it wasn't on the surface. It *was* the surface.

But was it ancient?

In 1988, scientists were given permission to test the cloth using radiocarbon dating. Samples were sent to three labs. The result stunned believers: the linen dated to between 1260 and 1390 CE.

Medieval. Not ancient.

That seemed like the final answer.

But then more questions arose.

Critics pointed out that the tested corner may have been repaired after the 1532 fire—possibly with newer threads. Others noted that bacteria, mold, and centuries of handling could have altered the cloth's chemistry. Could the test have dated the patch, not the whole shroud?

Meanwhile, new technologies revealed more.

In 1978, a group of American scientists known as the STURP team (Shroud of Turin Research Project) examined the cloth using imaging, spectroscopy, and ultraviolet light. They found no evidence of paint, brush strokes, or pigments. The image had 3D qualities—not something a painter could produce. And the blood, they said, *was* real.

But again, science hit a wall.

No one could explain how the image got there.

Some said it was a natural reaction from body heat or oils. Others suggested a burst of radiation—or something still unknown. None of the experiments so far have reproduced the effect.

The image isn't just art. It's not quite science. It's something in between. So what are the theories?

Some believe it's authentic: the real burial shroud of Jesus, bearing the imprint of his crucified body. Others say it's a brilliant medieval fake—created not to deceive, but to inspire.

Some believe it was made by Leonardo da Vinci using a primitive photographic technique. Others point to earlier depictions of the shroud in Byzantine art—arguing that the image existed long before the radiocarbon date.

Still others say it's a naturally formed image—something science hasn't fully understood yet.

In recent years, high-resolution scans, digital modeling, and pollen analysis have added more data—but not more certainty.

No one has definitively proven it's real. No one has definitively proven it's not. That's the paradox of the Shroud.

It inspires faith. It invites skepticism. And it defies easy explanation. Today, it's kept in a climate-controlled case in the Cathedral of Saint John the Baptist in Turin. It's rarely shown to the public. But millions have seen it—up close or in photos—and walked away with the same question:

What kind of mystery lasts 2,000 years?

The Shroud of Turin might be the oldest unsolved image in the world.

And it's still watching us.

THE GREEN CHILDREN OF WOOLPIT

What mysterious world did the Green Children come from?

How did they end up in Woolpit?

It was harvest time when they appeared.

Two children—a boy and a girl—stood at the edge of a deep pit near the village of Woolpit, England. They were wearing strange clothes. They spoke a language no one could recognize.

And their skin was green.

Not sickly. Not bruised. Green.

The villagers were stunned. The children looked frightened but alive. No one knew where they had come from. They weren't injured. Just confused, starving—and green.

What followed became one of the strangest mysteries in medieval history.

Two children, no known origin, no shared language with the people around them, and no explanation that ever quite made sense.

The only clues come from two written accounts, both decades later. One from a historian named William of Newburgh. The other from Ralph of Coggeshall, a monk who may have spoken with someone who saw the children firsthand.

Their stories overlap—but not perfectly. Which makes the whole case feel even stranger.

According to both accounts, the children were discovered near one of the village's large wolf pits (which is where Woolpit gets its name). Some villagers thought the kids had just climbed out of the earth itself.

They were taken in by a local landowner. At first, they refused to eat. Everything offered to them—bread, meat, vegetables—they rejected. Then someone brought green beans, still in the pod. They devoured them.

After that, their diet slowly expanded. The boy, described as the younger of the two, never fully recovered. He became sick and died within months.

But the girl survived. As she learned English, her green color faded. And her story—told only after she could speak clearly—was even stranger than her arrival.

She said they came from a place of perpetual twilight, where the sun never rose high in the sky. Everyone there was green. They lived underground or in a place separated from the world by a river of light. She said they had heard a strange sound while tending their father's cattle and followed it—into darkness, then into sunlight.

That's when they appeared near the pit.

She didn't know how they had gotten to Woolpit. She didn't even know what Woolpit was. She said she and her brother were just as shocked as the villagers had been.

People tried to explain it.

One theory was that they had wandered in from a nearby village where foreign workers lived—maybe Flemish refugees speaking a different language. Maybe they were malnourished, and the green skin came from anemia. Maybe they were just lost children with a strange story who had eaten too many green beans.

But other details didn't line up.

The girl's descriptions of her homeland didn't match anywhere in England. There were no missing persons reports that matched two green-skinned children. And their sudden appearance near a deep pit—without footprints, without anyone seeing where they came from—still made people whisper.

Some pointed to legends of fairy folk, who were said to live underground and sometimes let children wander into the human world. Others said it was a Christian allegory written down too literally. Still others insisted it was true and unexplained.

After the boy died, the girl was baptized and eventually worked in a nobleman's household. According to one account, she was "wanton and impudent"—which could mean she had adjusted to the culture around her. She eventually married and lived out her life in England.

But the mystery never faded.

Who were they? Where did they really come from? Why was their skin green? Why didn't they recognize the sun? Why did they only eat beans?

Why didn't the girl try to go home?

And how do two children appear from nowhere, speaking no known language, wearing no familiar clothes, and still leave behind no real evidence of who they were?

The landowner who took them in didn't seem to find a clear answer. The writers who recorded the tale decades later couldn't agree on the details. And modern historians can't explain it without asking more questions than they answer.

Two children walked out of the woods near a wolf pit.

Only one lived long enough to tell the story.

The words she gave us didn't solve the mystery. They deepened it.

And every year that passes makes it harder to explain.

The story remains—not buried, not debunked—just waiting.

Let's trace the records, weigh the accounts, and listen again to the strange voice that once came from the edge of the field.

THE
HOLY
GRAIL

What exactly is the Holy Grail?

Is it a real object, or could it be something more symbolic?

It doesn't appear in the Bible. No ancient scroll lists its location. No museum holds it.

And yet, the Holy Grail remains one of the most sought-after relics in history.

A cup. A symbol. A mystery.

Let's follow the clues.

The first known mention of the Grail appears in a French poem around 1180 CE. In it, a knight named Perceval stumbles upon a castle where a glowing vessel is carried in a sacred procession. The object is never fully explained. The poet, Chrétien de Troyes, died before finishing the tale.

That's clue number one: the Grail enters history already unfinished.

Soon after, new stories emerged.

In later versions of the Arthurian legends, the Grail becomes the holiest object in the realm—linked directly to Jesus. Some said it was the cup used at the Last Supper. Others claimed it caught Christ's blood during the crucifixion. It was said to heal the sick, grant eternal life, and only reveal itself to the pure of heart.

The stories changed, but one theme stayed the same: the Grail was never easy to find.

It wasn't just an object. It was a test.

So—could it be real?

Across Europe, churches claimed to hold the *true* Grail. One in Valencia, Spain, houses a simple stone cup with a long line of defenders. Other contenders appeared in England, Italy, and even Armenia. But none have been confirmed, and most are medieval at best.

In the 1980s, a bold new theory emerged: that the Grail wasn't a cup at all, but a code. A secret passed down through generations. According to this view—made famous by *The Da Vinci Code*—the Grail refers to the bloodline of Jesus, hidden for centuries and protected by secret societies.

It's an electrifying idea—but not one supported by historical evidence.

Still, even in older texts, the Grail takes different forms. In some it's a dish. In others, a stone. Sometimes it glows. Sometimes it disappears. It may have roots in both Christian and Celtic mythology—a blend of relic and symbol, hero's journey and holy vision.

So what was it really?

A literal relic? A forgotten tradition? A metaphor for spiritual enlightenment?

The truth may be this: the Grail is powerful precisely because it isn't pinned down. It's part relic, part riddle. Every age redefines it. Every seeker brings their own hopes to the search.

And that's the final clue.

Because the Grail's power doesn't come from being found. It comes from being *sought*.

The quest itself—the courage, faith, failure, and change along the way—is what gives the Grail its meaning.

Whether it sits in a vault, a cave, a chapel… or nowhere at all.

It's the mystery that lasts. And the search that never ends.

EL DORADO

Where is the legendary city of El Dorado?

What happened to all those explorers who journeyed into the wilds of South America in search of its treasures?

I t started with a man covered in gold.

Spanish explorers in South America heard whispers of a tribal leader who coated himself in gold dust, sailed into the middle of a lake, and washed it off as an offering to the gods.

They called him El Hombre Dorado—the golden man.

But the story didn't stay small for long.

The golden man became a golden city. Then a kingdom. Then an entire empire hidden deep in the jungle, filled with temples, palaces, and rivers lined with treasure.

They called it El Dorado.

And thousands of men died trying to find it.

The first clues came from the Muisca people of Colombia. They did hold gold ceremonies at Lake Guatavita, where a new chief made offerings by boat. Spanish soldiers later tried to drain the lake. They found a few gold artifacts—but not the mountain of treasure they expected.

That only made them more certain it existed.

Over the next century, the legend of El Dorado drifted across the continent. Every time a search failed, the city moved. Some said it lay beyond the Andes. Others claimed it was hidden in the Amazon. Some insisted it was protected by spirits or jungle magic.

In the 1590s, Sir Walter Raleigh led expeditions to find it. He returned to England full of stories—pillars of gold, golden-roofed temples, a massive inland lake. But he came back empty-handed. His failure cost him his reputation, and eventually, his life.

Still, the stories kept spreading.

Each explorer described something different: cities with golden streets, temples lined in gems, or kings who threw emeralds into rivers like skipping stones. The lack of proof didn't kill the legend—it just pushed it deeper into the unknown.

So was El Dorado ever real?

Not exactly.

But it wasn't entirely fake, either.

The gold ritual at Lake Guatavita was real. The Muisca culture, their goldwork, and their sacred traditions have all been confirmed through archaeology. What wasn't real was the European fantasy: a literal city built of gold bricks.

But here's where it gets interesting.

Modern scientists are now discovering that massive civilizations did exist deep in the Amazon. Buried under jungle growth for centuries, these cities had roads, canals, plazas, and housing for tens of thousands of people.

No treasure has been found—but the scale and complexity are stunning.

El Dorado may have been a myth, but like many legends, it was built around a sliver of truth. Real rituals. Real gold. Real people. Just told and retold until the details bent out of shape.

A dust-covered king. A shining lake.
A name passed from explorer to explorer, growing heavier with each retelling.

The city may never have existed.
But the obsession it created was very real.

CROP CIRCLES

Where do crop circles come from, and how do these incredibly detailed patterns appear overnight?

Could there be a hidden message in these mysterious designs?

I t starts overnight.

One day, a farmer looks out across a field of wheat or barley—perfect rows stretching to the horizon. The next morning, something's changed.

The stalks are flattened. But not broken.

They're bent gently, forming circles. Or rings. Or spirals. Or sometimes complex shapes hundreds of feet wide— geometric, precise, and eerily perfect. No tire tracks. No footprints. No explanation.

Just a message no one can read.

Let's follow the clues.

Crop circles started gaining attention in the 1970s in the English countryside. Most appeared in southern England— especially Wiltshire, near ancient sites like Stonehenge and Avebury. But reports soon spread to other parts of the world: Canada, Australia, Germany, the U.S.

At first, they were simple circles. One or two rings, always appearing overnight. Scientists investigated the soil. Photographers flew overhead. Paranormal researchers showed up with Geiger counters.

And then the shapes evolved.

Over time, circles turned into chains, then spirals, then shapes resembling DNA, mathematical formulas, even three-dimensional cubes viewed from above.

The more people studied them, the more complex they became.

That's clue #1.

Were these messages?

If so, who—or *what*—was sending them?

Some believed they were caused by natural phenomena— wind patterns, strange whirlwinds, plasma vortexes. Others claimed they were made by aliens, trying to communicate through symbols. A few pointed to military experiments or classified tech that left invisible footprints in the crops.

Then came 1991.

Two men—Doug Bower and Dave Chorley—stepped forward in England and admitted they had made hundreds of the circles using planks, ropes, and careful stomping. They even demonstrated how they did it. The media declared the mystery solved.

Case closed?

Not quite.

Because after Doug and Dave came clean, the circles didn't stop.

They got stranger.

More intricate. More widespread. Designs appeared with stunning complexity, in fields that had no sign of human entry. Stalks weren't snapped or trampled—they were gently bent at the nodes, often in patterns that rotated clockwise in some parts and counterclockwise in others.

Some researchers noted magnetic particles fused in the soil, or changes in the crystalline structure of the plants themselves.

That's clue #2.

If pranksters were making all of them, how were they pulling off 600-foot mandalas in pitch darkness without mistakes—or leaving a trace?

In 2001, a formation appeared near the Chilbolton radio telescope in England. It resembled a reply to the Arecibo message—an encoded signal humans had broadcast into space in 1974 to announce our presence. The crop formation mimicked the structure of the original signal but changed key parts—adding a different DNA code, a different solar system, and an image of a large-headed being.

A few days later, a second formation appeared nearby: a face. Coincidence? Hoax? Or something else? The debate continues.

Some scientists dismiss all crop circles as man-made art—clever, but explainable. And yes, many formations *have* been proven hoaxes. Some were made for advertising campaigns. Others were built by artist collectives using GPS, ladders, and even drones.

But that still leaves a handful of cases where something doesn't add up. The speed. The silence. The bent, not broken, stalks. The lack of physical evidence. And, occasionally, the strange reports: locals who say they saw lights in the sky. Heard buzzing. Lost time.

And one more detail: the best formations often appear near ancient sacred sites—stone circles, ley lines, hill figures.

That's clue #3. Is it chance? Or is someone—or something—drawing these shapes on land already charged with meaning? We may never know for sure.

The idea of shapes appearing in fields goes back further than most realize. A woodcut from 1678—called the "Mowing Devil"—shows a demonic figure carving a circle in a field after a farmer refused to pay a worker's wages. Whether that's satire or an early sighting, no one knows.

But one thing is certain: Crop circles capture the imagination because they're silent, sudden, and strange.

Even if they're all hoaxes, they're still worth asking about. Who's making them? Why are they so beautiful? And why do they keep appearing in places tied to ancient myth?

Maybe they're modern art. Maybe they're coded messages. Maybe they're just very well-planned jokes. But they're still happening...

And no one knows why.

THE BLOOD RAIN OF KERALA

What makes rain
turn red? Why does
this happen in Kerala,
but not in other places?

Are there creatures or
chemicals in the air
that could cause this
spooky red color?

I t began with a stain.

On July 25, 2001, people in the Indian state of Kerala looked up to see red rain falling from the sky. It hit rooftops. Splattered on white clothing. Soaked into the soil. Locals said it looked like blood.

And it wasn't a one-time event.

For nearly two months, red rain fell off and on across the region. Sometimes it was pink. Sometimes dark scarlet. In some towns, leaves turned black. Wells changed color. People whispered about omens, pollution—even supernatural punishment.

But the mystery had only begun.

Let's follow the clues.

First, the red wasn't from dust or rust. This wasn't just dirty water. It stained permanently. And when scientists collected samples, they found something strange: the rain was filled with microscopic particles—round, cell-like structures. About 4–10 microns wide. They looked biological. Almost like spores.

That was clue #1.

At first, Indian scientists believed the red particles might be from algae or a type of mold. But where had it come from? Some suggested local trees or lichen releasing spores in large numbers. But there was no evidence of a bloom big enough to explain it.

Then came the second theory: a meteor.

Just before the red rain began, residents reported hearing a loud boom—possibly a small meteor exploding high in the atmosphere. Could it have delivered strange biological material? That idea caught the attention of researchers at Mahatma Gandhi University, who began testing the particles.

That led to clue #2.

The particles weren't toxic. They weren't bacteria. They didn't contain DNA—or if they did, it was in a form scientists couldn't detect. When heated to over 300°C, they didn't break down.

That's when a bold theory emerged: these particles might not be from Earth.

Two researchers proposed that the red rain was an example of panspermia—the idea that life, or the building blocks of life, can travel through space and seed planets. If a meteor had carried these strange spores from space, it might explain their durability—and their sudden appearance.

But the theory was controversial.

Most scientists rejected it. Later studies argued that the red rain was caused by a local species of airborne algae. The particles did contain DNA, they said—just not in high amounts.

But not everyone was convinced.

Why did the rain last for weeks? Why did it appear in patches across hundreds of kilometers? And what about the initial meteor sound?

There's still no complete answer.

Even today, the Blood Rain of Kerala sits on the edge of science—a blend of biology, mystery, and cosmic possibility. Whether the cause was earthly or not, the red rain left behind a permanent question mark.

It fell without warning. It left no clear trace. And it reminded us that even the sky can bleed.

MYSTERY AIRSHIP

Why did the Mystery
Airship appear all over the
place, and why did it vanish
just as mysteriously?

Who were the people who
flew it, and what were they
trying to do?

I t began in 1896.

A strange light appeared in the skies over Sacramento, California—moving slowly, silently, against the wind. Some said it had wings. Others described a long, cigar-shaped body with a powerful spotlight on the front.

Within days, people across the state were seeing the same thing. Newspapers called it an "airship."

But airplanes hadn't been invented yet.

Over the next year, the sightings spread east—across the Midwest, over Texas, even as far as New York. Hundreds of witnesses, from farmers to judges to sheriffs, described a flying craft unlike anything known to science.

Some said it made mechanical noises, like clanking gears. Others claimed it hovered. A few swore they saw human pilots aboard—sometimes waving, sometimes shouting instructions in strange languages.

And then it was gone.

No wreckage. No crash. No inventor ever came forward.

Just newspaper clippings, public confusion, and one giant question:

What were people seeing?

At the time, the Wright brothers were still years away from their first flight. Balloons existed, but they drifted on the wind. Zeppelins hadn't yet been built. Nothing on record could explain a machine flying under control across the country.

The airship wasn't just a rumor. The reports were detailed and surprisingly consistent. Many witnesses described the same shape: a narrow body, fixed wings, sometimes fins, and powerful lights. Some even gave dimensions—over 100 feet long, with room for passengers.

In several towns, groups of people watched it for minutes at a time. Horses reportedly panicked. Dogs howled. Some sightings lasted over an hour.

The press went wild. Sketches appeared in papers nationwide. Editorials debated whether it was a hoax, a secret military craft, or something far stranger.

And then things got weirder.

A few witnesses claimed they spoke with the pilots.

In one account, a man said the airship crew told him they were American inventors, testing a flying machine in secret. Another claimed the pilot said he was from another planet. These stories were often printed with a wink—but they were printed.

Skeptics dismissed it all as mass hysteria or newspaper exaggeration. Some accused local pranksters. Others said people were seeing Venus, meteors, or even migrating birds lit by city lights.

But those explanations didn't account for the same shape being seen across thousands of miles, by people who had never met.

Then, in 1897, the sightings stopped. Just like that.

Some believe the airship was a prototype that was scrapped or lost. Others think it was all a hoax fueled by copycat stories and media hype.

No physical evidence was ever found. No plans. No engines. Just paper trails.

But something was in the skies.

And for one strange year, Americans looked up—and saw a machine that wasn't supposed to exist.

AMELIA EARHART

How could one of the world's most famous pilots disappear without a trace?

Did Amelia Earhart and her navigator, Fred Noonan, crash into the ocean, or did they somehow survive on a remote island?

LAE

LAST KNOWN POSITION

HOWLAND ISLAND

40

35

30

34

LINE NORTH
157-337

July 2, 1937. 8:43 a.m. local time.

Amelia Earhart's voice crackled over the radio: *"We are on the line 157-337, running north and south."*

And then… nothing.

No more messages. No distress call. No confirmed wreckage. Just a flat ocean and a trail that vanished into open air.

She had been flying for over 20 hours. It was the most dangerous leg of her round-the-world attempt—2,500 miles from New Guinea to a tiny Pacific island called Howland. A U.S. Coast Guard ship, the *Itasca*, was stationed nearby to guide her in.

They never saw her plane.

Amelia Earhart was one of the most famous people in the world. She'd flown solo across the Atlantic. She'd broken records, written books, and inspired a generation of girls to look up instead of down. She wasn't reckless. She was smart, careful, and strategic. Which made her disappearance all the more baffling.

She was flying a Lockheed Electra, a twin-engine aircraft outfitted with custom long-range fuel tanks. Her navigator, Fred Noonan, was one of the best in the business. They'd mapped their course meticulously. They had backup plans. They had training. What they didn't have was radar, GPS, or satellite rescue. One wrong move in the Pacific, and there was nothing but water.

Radio messages from that morning suggest she was close to Howland Island—close enough to see the ship's smoke signal, but not close enough to locate it. The *Itasca* heard her transmissions, but she didn't seem to hear theirs. The signals faded. The sky stayed empty.

A massive search effort began within hours. Ships and planes swept 250,000 square miles of ocean. Nothing was found. No debris. No oil slick. No bodies. No signal. Just a few final radio messages, fading into silence.

So what happened?

That question has fueled nearly a century of theories—and a long list of clues that never quite add up.

The most official theory is the simplest: she ran out of fuel and ditched into the ocean. That part of the Pacific is unimaginably vast. A small silver plane would sink in seconds. If that's what happened, the wreckage may never be found.

But that's not the only possibility.

Some researchers believe she missed Howland Island by a few miles and turned south, looking for another strip of land called **Nikumaroro**. In the weeks after her disappearance, shortwave radio operators around the world claimed to hear faint signals—pleas for help in a woman's voice. One message reportedly said the plane was "part on land, part in water." The messages faded after a few days, as high tide may have swept the wreckage away.

Years later, search teams visited Nikumaroro and found a piece of aircraft aluminum, a woman's shoe, and a compact mirror—possibly from the 1930s. A skeleton was discovered in 1940, but later lost. A bone analysis from old measurements suggests it may have belonged to a woman of Earhart's build. Nothing definitive. But just enough to keep the question alive.

Other theories go darker.

Some believe she crashed in the Japanese-controlled Marshall Islands and was captured. One photo, now discredited, claimed to show her sitting on a dock in Japanese custody. Others suggest she was forced to spy, assumed a new identity, or secretly returned to the U.S. and lived in hiding. These theories are harder to prove—and easier to sensationalize—but they won't fully disappear.

Meanwhile, deep-sea sonar teams have scanned the seafloor near Howland Island. In 2019, a high-tech expedition mapped thousands of square miles. Still nothing.

So what's the truth?

A skilled pilot. A clear flight plan. A navigator with decades of experience. A final transmission at 8:43 a.m.

Then—no signal, no splash, no wreckage.

Just an open sky, a dark ocean, and one of the sharpest minds in aviation history, lost on a routine morning in July.

The facts remain. The answers don't.

But somewhere between that last radio message and the empty silence that followed, something happened. And whatever it was,
no one was ready for it.

MIRACLE
OF THE SUN

What made the sun appear to move
and dance in the sky that day in 1917?

How did three young shepherd
children end up at the center of one of
the world's most famous miracles?

It was raining that morning.

A cold, steady October rain soaked the countryside of Fátima, Portugal. Tens of thousands of people gathered in the muddy fields near the Cova da Iria, waiting in silence. Some had walked for miles. Others came on crutches, carrying their sick. Many were soaked, exhausted, and skeptical.

They had come to see a miracle.

And just after noon, something happened.

The rain stopped. The clouds broke. And then, according to dozens of witnesses, the sun began to move.

Let's follow the clues.

The date was October 13, 1917. The world was still at war. But in this small village, something very different was unfolding. For six months, three shepherd children—Lucia, Jacinta, and Francisco—had claimed that a woman "brighter than the sun" had appeared to them. They said she was sent by God, and she gave them visions, warnings, and promises.

She told them she would perform a miracle on October 13, so that all would believe.

Word spread fast. By the time the day arrived, estimates say between 30,000 and 70,000 people had gathered in the fields.

And that's when it happened.

Witnesses said the clouds parted and the sun appeared as a dull, silver disc. They said it spun in the sky like a wheel of fire. It changed colors. It danced. Then, according to hundreds of people, it plunged toward the Earth in a zigzag motion—terrifying the crowd—before suddenly returning to its place in the sky.

Clue #1: the crowd was not all believers.

Journalists, skeptics, even scientists were there—and many said the same thing. A reporter from O Século, a major Portuguese newspaper, wrote that he saw the sun "whirl and dance" in a way that defied natural explanation.

Clue #2: some people saw nothing.

A few observers—especially those farther away—saw only the sky clear or the sun shine briefly. No motion. No color change. This has led some to suggest that the event was psychological—a mass hallucination triggered by expectation.

But that theory doesn't fully explain the shared details in so many eyewitness reports. Or the fact that, immediately after the event, the previously soaked ground and clothes were suddenly dry.

Clue #3: the predictions were specific.

Lucia, the oldest of the children, told people the miracle would happen around noon. And it did—within minutes. That kind of accuracy makes it harder to dismiss as chance or weather coincidence.

So what are the theories?

Some scientists have suggested a rare optical phenomenon called a "sun halo" or "parhelion," where ice crystals in the upper atmosphere refract sunlight into bright, spinning circles. But most such effects don't involve rapid, zigzagging motion—or sudden drying of wet clothing and mud.

Others point to retinal afterimages or eye damage from staring at the sun too long. But many observers reported seeing the event clearly without discomfort—and described it in motion, not as a fixed glare.

Then there's the religious view.

The Catholic Church officially declared the event a miracle in 1930. The children's visions—later known as the "Secrets of Fátima"—became the subject of global fascination. The Church did not claim the sun literally moved, but that God used a natural phenomenon for a divine purpose.

Skeptics argue that the event can be explained without invoking the supernatural.

Believers say the timing, the scale, and the impact make that unlikely.

The truth may lie somewhere in between.

The "Miracle of the Sun" didn't leave behind photos or film. It wasn't measured with instruments. But it lives in testimony—thousands of voices saying something impossible happened that day.

Something that couldn't be explained.

And here's the most enduring clue: people didn't just witness the event. Many were changed by it. Some were healed. Some converted. Even the government, once hostile to the children, backed off.

So what happened over Fátima that day?

A miracle? A rare optical event? A moment of shared faith?

Maybe all three.

Whatever it was, it wasn't expected.

It wasn't recorded by weather stations.

And it hasn't happened again.

The children said the Lady came with a warning—about war, about the world, about the need to pray.

But the sun—dancing, spinning, falling—was the moment the world noticed.

And whether you believe or doubt, one fact remains:

Tens of thousands of people saw something.

And none of them ever forgot it.

THE
FAIRY
CIRCLES
OF NAMIBIA

What could make almost perfect
circles appear in the ground?

Why are these circles so consistent
and long-lasting, especially in a
harsh desert?

Fly over the desert of Namibia, and you'll see them. Thousands of circles—bare patches of reddish dirt, each ringed by tall grass. From above, they stretch to the horizon like a field of ancient coins or the dotted skin of some massive, sleeping beast.

No fences. No roads. No ruins.

Just empty circles.
Perfectly round.
And no one knows exactly why they're there.

Let's follow the clues.

These strange formations—called fairy circles—appear across hundreds of miles of desert grassland, mainly in southern Angola and northern Namibia. Each one is about 10 to 30 feet wide. Nothing grows in the center. But the rim? Lush, green grass, fed by something unseen.

To local Himba communities, the circles are the footprints of gods. Or the resting places of dragons. The "fairies" in the name come from colonial legends—whispers of invisible beings making patterns while humans sleep.

But scientists don't deal in folklore.

So they started to dig.

Clue #1: there are no roots in the center of a fairy circle. Not dead ones. Not even dried-out remnants. It's not that plants die in the circle—they never grow there at all.

This led to one theory: termites.

Specifically, sand termites—*Psammotermes allocerus*. Some researchers found evidence of these insects living beneath the circles, feeding on grass roots and slowly clearing the area. Without roots to hold moisture, water collects under the bare patch, creating a kind of underground reservoir. The ring of grass around the circle benefits from that extra water.

It's a compelling theory. Termites make sense.

But not everyone agrees.

Clue #2: many circles have no termites. Or they do—but so does the rest of the field. Why would termites create perfect circles in some spots and not others? And why are the shapes so mathematically consistent?

That brings us to another idea: self-organization.

In harsh deserts, water is everything. Some scientists suggest that the grasses themselves are arranging into patterns. When a few plants begin to outcompete others for moisture, they force gaps to form. Those gaps grow, ringed by grasses that benefit from the water that collects nearby. Over time, a feedback loop creates regular, repeating patterns across the land.

It's a natural system—plants shaping their own environment like raindrops carving a canyon.

Computer models support this idea. Similar patterns appear in chemical reactions, coral reefs, even galaxies.

But still—why circles? Why here?

And why do they vanish?

Clue #3: fairy circles are temporary. After several decades, they fade. New ones appear nearby. Satellite images show this slow migration over time—like the land is breathing.

They also exist in only a few places. Namibia. Parts of Australia. Nowhere else.

So are they caused by insects?

By plants?

By both?

Some now believe it's a combination: termites creating one kind of stress, grasses responding in another. One circle may be mostly biological. Another, mostly ecological. The result is the same—a strange ring with a blank middle, holding the desert's secrets in silence.

And that brings us to the final mystery.

Fairy circles aren't ancient ruins. They aren't created by machines or meteorites. There's no buried stone, no radiation, no footprints.

Just emptiness.

Measured. Repeating. Mysterious.

You can walk into one and feel nothing.

But stand still, and you'll notice how quiet it is.

The air hangs differently. The grass holds a shape. The land keeps its pattern.

That's what draws people in—not because they expect answers, but because the question is still alive.

Why circles?

Why here?

And why now?

Maybe the clues aren't all underground.

Maybe they're in the way systems form.

The way competition creates balance.

Or maybe, like so many mysteries, the fairy circles aren't asking to be solved.

They're asking us to observe.

Because sometimes, the land itself holds the pen.

And we're just beginning to read what it's written.

MYSTERY OF
MARY CELESTE

ALL WELL

What could make an entire crew
vanish without a trace?

Why was a perfectly sound ship left
drifting, as if frozen in time?

It was a calm December afternoon in 1872 when the crew of the British ship *Dei Gratia* spotted something strange drifting through the Atlantic.

A brigantine, sails fluttering, about 600 miles west of Portugal. No signal. No distress flag. Just... there.

Captain David Morehouse knew the ship. It was the *Mary Celeste*, an American merchant vessel that had left New York eight days before he did, carrying 1,700 barrels of industrial alcohol bound for Genoa. He'd dined with her captain, Benjamin Briggs, before departure.

Now she was bobbing eerily in open water, off-course and silent.

The *Dei Gratia* pulled alongside. A small boarding party was sent over. What they found would become one of the most enduring maritime mysteries of all time.

The ship was **abandoned**.

No sign of a struggle. No bodies. No blood. The lifeboat was gone, but everything else was strangely... normal.

Food and water stores were untouched. The crew's clothes were still in their chests. There was a sewing machine left out, a child's toy on the captain's bed. Captain Briggs, his wife Sarah, and their two-year-old daughter Sophia were missing— along with the seven-man crew.

But the strangest part?

The ship was still seaworthy.

The sails were tattered and a little out of trim. A few hatch covers were off. The single pump in the hold had a little water in it—but not enough to sink her. The navigation tools were missing, and the ship's log had been oddly stopped ten days earlier. The last entry said they were near the Azores.

That's where the clues end.

Nothing about the ship's condition explained why the crew would **abandon it mid-ocean** in a perfectly good vessel and take their chances in a single lifeboat. Especially with a child on board. Especially when the nearest land was hundreds of miles away.

When the *Mary Celeste* was brought to Gibraltar for investigation, maritime authorities scratched their heads. Piracy? Mutiny? Poison? A seaquake? They found a sword with some discoloration on it—originally reported as blood—but later proven to be rust. Some barrels of alcohol had leaked. That was it.

Over time, theories multiplied.

One suggested the leaking alcohol gave off **toxic fumes**, leading the crew to panic and abandon ship, fearing an explosion. But no signs of fire or damage were found. Others suggested a sudden **waterspout or seaquake** made the ship appear to be sinking, prompting a hasty exit. Again, no real evidence.

More outlandish explanations included **giant squid**, **alien abduction**, or even a secret plot to fake the crew's death. None of them explained why the lifeboat was never found and why there wasn't even a single scrap of wreckage from it.

Then there's the theory about Captain Briggs himself. Some say he could have gone mad and done something unthinkable—but those who knew him described him as deeply religious, steady, and responsible. He had even brought his wife and toddler on the trip. It made no sense.

The ship's cargo was intact. No signs of theft. No evidence that anyone had profited from the disappearance.

As the years passed, the name *Mary Celeste* became a kind of shorthand for vanishing without a trace. The case inspired dozens of novels, films, and fictional accounts—including one early short story by Arthur Conan Doyle that was so convincing, many people mistook it for a true explanation.

In 1885, the ship met a bizarre end of its own—deliberately wrecked in a staged insurance fraud. But by then, the mystery had already taken on a life of its own.

What really happened in those gray-blue waves west of Portugal?

Why would a trained crew and seasoned captain leave a safe ship?

Why didn't anyone try to return?

There were no storms that day. No pirates. No sign of disease or sabotage. Only one lifeboat vanished into the sea—taking every explanation with it.

In a world of shipwrecks, the *Mary Celeste* wasn't broken.
In a century of disasters, this one left no bodies.
Only questions, drifting behind her like a wake.

THE CURSE OF
KING TUT'S TOMB

Could a curse really doom anyone
who enters a tomb?

Was it all just bad luck, or
something even stranger?

When they opened the tomb, the air inside hadn't moved in over 3,000 years.

It was November 1922. After years of digging in the scorching Valley of the Kings, British archaeologist Howard Carter stood at the sealed doorway of a forgotten tomb—one that hadn't been looted in ancient times, one that might actually be intact.

He held up a candle and peered inside through a small hole in the door.

His words became famous: *"Yes, wonderful things."*

He had found the tomb of **Tutankhamun**, a young pharaoh who had ruled Egypt for less than a decade and died before his 20th birthday. His name had been lost to time. But inside the tomb were golden statues, thrones, chariots, weapons, and a coffin made of solid gold. Nothing like it had ever been seen before.

It was the greatest archaeological find in modern history.

And then people started dying.

Just a few months after the tomb was opened, Lord Carnarvon—the man who financed the dig—fell ill. He had been bitten by a mosquito on his cheek. The bite got infected. He died of blood poisoning in a Cairo hospital.

At the exact moment of his death, lights reportedly went out across the city.

Back in England, Carnarvon's dog howled and collapsed. She died, too.

Newspapers jumped on the story. They began calling it **"The Curse of the Pharaoh."** Reporters claimed that anyone who entered the tomb would suffer the consequences.

More deaths followed.

An American millionaire who visited the tomb died of pneumonia. Another member of the expedition dropped dead of blood poisoning. One of Carter's close friends collapsed while shaving. The man who X-rayed Tutankhamun's mummy died within months. The list kept growing.

Some tallied more than a **dozen mysterious deaths** linked to the discovery. Sudden illnesses. Accidents. Fevers. Strokes. Not all were at the site. Some occurred years later, across oceans. But the rumors didn't care.

People whispered that ancient magic had been disturbed. That the tomb had been sealed for a reason. That Tutankhamun's soul had been awakened.

One of the strangest details was found inside the burial chamber itself.

Carved into the wall of the tomb's antechamber, there was said to be a warning: *"Death shall come on swift wings to him who disturbs the king."* Carter never confirmed this. No such inscription was officially recorded. But that didn't stop people from repeating it.

Not everyone believed in the curse.

Skeptics pointed out that Howard Carter himself—the man who opened the tomb—lived for another 17 years. So did many of his staff. In fact, most of the key archaeologists survived well into old age.

Some scientists say the deaths could be explained by mold or bacteria sealed inside the tomb. After centuries without oxygen or light, dangerous spores may have been released when the tomb was opened. That theory remains unproven.

Others believe it was pure coincidence. A mix of tropical diseases, infections, and the rough conditions of early 20th-century fieldwork.

Still, the deaths were real. The fear was real. And the legend took root.

Even today, the idea of the "mummy's curse" shows up in books, movies, games, and museum tours. People avoid walking under ladders. They throw salt over their shoulders. And they hesitate—just a little—before staring too long into the hollow eyes of a pharaoh's mask.

Tutankhamun was a minor king in his own time. But his tomb, untouched and glittering with treasures, made him immortal.

The boy king did not build pyramids. He ruled briefly, then died young, buried in haste.

But someone sealed his tomb with care. Someone left behind a chamber filled with gold and gods.

And someone made sure it stayed hidden until the world was ready to open the door—and face whatever waited inside.

The artifacts were studied. The treasures were removed. The body was unwrapped.

The clues were documented.

And the silence inside that tomb? It didn't last long.

THE
PHAISTOS DISC

Who created this strange disc, covered with mysterious symbols?

What secrets does it hold? Was it meant to pass down hidden knowledge or reveal a code lost to time?

It looks like something left behind by a civilization we've never met.

A disc, about six inches wide. Flat, round, made of clay. Spirals of stamped symbols coil across both sides—over two hundred in total. Tiny figures. Arrows. Flowers. Shields. A helmet. A running man. A winged insect.

Each symbol was carefully pressed into the wet clay using carved stamps—long before the age of printing presses or typewriters.

It's called the **Phaistos Disc**, and it shouldn't exist.

Because it was made more than 3,500 years ago, in a world where written language was still rare, and where no one else left behind anything remotely like it.

It was discovered in 1908 by an Italian archaeologist digging beneath the ruins of an ancient palace on the island of Crete. The site was called Phaistos. Most of what had been uncovered there belonged to the Minoan civilization, a mysterious Bronze Age culture known for its massive palaces, elaborate art, and undeciphered scripts.

But this disc didn't match anything else found in the ruins—not the language, not the method, not the purpose.

It was a complete one-off.

No duplicates. No copies. No companion tablets. Just one disc, pressed with strange stamped symbols and fired in a kiln.

It's currently held in a museum in Heraklion, Greece. Scholars have been staring at it for over a hundred years. No one can read it.

The disc is about as big as a compact disc or small plate. On each side, a line of symbols winds inward in a tight spiral, as if it's meant to be read from the outer edge toward the center. There are 241 symbols in total, made from 45 unique characters. Each was stamped—one by one—into the clay while it was still soft. Once the disc was complete, it was baked, turning it into a hard, permanent artifact.

This wasn't someone doodling in the dirt. It was planned, printed, and preserved.

And no one has a clue what it says.

Some experts believe it's a prayer. Others think it's a list of names, a record, or a ceremonial hymn. A few say it could be a board game, a coded message, or even a form of proto-computer logic. But those are just guesses. No Rosetta Stone has ever been found for these symbols. Nothing like this disc has ever turned up again—on Crete or anywhere else in the ancient world.

The Minoans did have writing systems. One is called **Linear A**, which has never been deciphered. Another, **Linear B**, was decoded in the 1950s and turned out to be an early form of Greek—but the Phaistos Disc doesn't match either of those.

It uses pictographic symbols—tiny drawings that seem to represent ideas or sounds. Some are repeated in patterns, suggesting syllables or grammar. But without a known language to compare it to, it's like solving a crossword with no clues and half the letters missing.

Many attempts have been made. Some researchers have claimed partial translations. Others insist the disc is a hoax from the early 1900s—though the clay and firing method match the Bronze Age. No serious evidence has ever proven it was faked.

The disc's layout is particularly strange. Most ancient writing moves in straight lines—left to right, or top to bottom. Spirals are rare. And stamping each character rather than carving by hand suggests the creator was trying to produce multiple copies—yet no others have ever been found.

Some scholars argue that the disc represents a lost writing system. Not Minoan, not Mycenaean, not Egyptian, not Sumerian—something else. A language spoken by a culture that left almost nothing else behind. A one-time message from a ghost civilization.

Or maybe it was an experiment. A new system someone tried, recorded once, and abandoned forever.

Until another example turns up—if one ever does—we won't know.

What we're left with is a riddle frozen in clay. A message written with care, pressed and fired, sealed and buried. It's survived wars, earthquakes, looters, and time itself.

But not understanding.

The disc remains untouched by translation. Its meaning is still sealed in silence.

And for now, that's all we've got.

BIGFOOT

Who, or what, is this mysterious creature?

What explains the massive footprints left in it wake?

What is to explain the numerous bigfoot sightings?

Start with the footprint.

A human-shaped track, 16 inches long, pressed deep into the mud of a forest trail. No claw marks. No shoes. Just five toes and a heavy step.

Then another.

And another.

Each spaced too far apart for a normal stride. No drag marks. No signs of trickery. Just a quiet trail vanishing into the trees.

That's usually where Bigfoot starts—not with a roar or a shadow, but with something left behind.

Let's follow the clues.

The legend of Bigfoot—also known as Sasquatch—goes back centuries. Indigenous tribes across North America told stories of large, hairy forest beings who walked upright, lived in remote mountains, and avoided humans. They were described as giants, spirits, or wild men of the woods.

That's clue #1: this isn't a new story.

In fact, the name "Sasquatch" comes from a Salish word: *Sésquac*, meaning "wild man." These tales existed long before the first European settlers arrived.

But in 1958, the legend stepped into the modern age.

A road construction crew in Bluff Creek, California, discovered enormous footprints around their worksite. A journalist named Andrew Genzoli published photos of the prints in the local paper. The story went viral. Letters poured in. People from all over claimed they'd seen something similar.

The creature was now called "Bigfoot." And the hunt was on.

Soon, more reports surfaced—across the Pacific Northwest and beyond. Hunters. Hikers. Campers. Police officers. Even trained biologists. They told similar stories: a large, upright creature—six to ten feet tall—covered in dark hair, with long arms, a massive stride, and glowing eyes in the dark.

Many also reported a smell—rank, sour, like rotting meat.

Then, in 1967, came the most famous piece of Bigfoot evidence: the Patterson-Gimlin film.

Shot near Bluff Creek—the same area as the original 1958 footprints—the short film shows a large, hairy creature walking upright, glancing back over its shoulder before disappearing into the trees.

To this day, the footage remains controversial.

Skeptics call it a hoax, claiming it was a man in a gorilla suit. Others argue the movement, muscle flexing, and proportions are too advanced for 1960s costume tech. Hollywood special effects artists have studied the film frame by frame—and remain divided.

That's clue #2: the film hasn't been proven fake. But it hasn't been proven real, either.

So what about physical evidence?

Over the years, thousands of alleged footprints have been cast in plaster. Some show dermal ridges—skin patterns like fingerprints. Others appear too clean, too staged. DNA samples have been collected from hair, scat, and scratches on trees—but so far, none have definitively come from an unknown species.

In some cases, the DNA turns out to be from bears. Or humans. Or dogs. In others, the samples are too degraded to identify.

And yet, the sightings keep coming.

From Washington state to rural Georgia. From the snowy woods of Alberta to the mountains of Oregon. Some reports are clearly fake. Some are cases of misidentified bears. But others are harder to explain—especially when witnesses have nothing to gain and everything to lose by speaking up.

Then there's the vocalization.

Several audio recordings claim to capture Bigfoot calls— whoops, howls, deep vocalizations unlike anything local animals make. Some wildlife experts say they could be elk or coyotes. Others say they're truly unknown.

That's clue #3: even without a body, the evidence hasn't stopped.

So what's the explanation?

Some scientists believe Bigfoot is a cultural myth—an expression of our ancient fear of the forest. Others think it's a case of misidentification layered over decades of storytelling. Still others propose it could be a relic hominid— something like *Gigantopithecus*, an extinct ape from Asia that may have crossed into North America during the Ice Age.

But no bones have been found. No fur. No bodies. No clear DNA. And that's the biggest gap in the case.

Because if Bigfoot is real—somewhere, at some point— one should have been found. Dead. Caught. Tracked. Tagged. But nothing definitive has ever surfaced.

Still, the forests are vast. And most sightings happen in remote, wild terrain. Maybe the creature is rare. Maybe it buries its dead. Maybe it doesn't want to be found.

Or maybe Bigfoot exists not in the trees—but in the space between folklore and fear.

A reflection of something deeper: our desire to believe that mystery still lives beyond the edge of the map.

Either way, it's never gone away. And something doesn't leave tracks unless it's been walking through.

THE
TUNGUSKA
EVENT

What really happened in the skies
over Tunguska that morning?

Why was there no impact crater,
no debris, no fragments left behind to
tell the tale?

The sky exploded just after breakfast.

June 30, 1908. Deep in the Siberian wilderness, near the Podkamennaya Tunguska River, a blinding flash of light streaked across the morning sky. Then came a shockwave so strong it flattened trees across more than 800 square miles. The blast knocked people off their feet 40 miles away. Windows shattered. Horses panicked. Some herders were thrown into the air.

And then, silence.

When the smoke cleared, a forest had been flattened into a giant ring—trees lying in perfect rows, all pointing away from a mysterious center.

Whatever had exploded didn't just hit the Earth. It rearranged it.

But when scientists finally arrived—years later—they found something even stranger.

There was no impact crater.

No chunks of rock. No obvious meteorite. Just scorched trees, bent soil, and a missing piece of the sky.

So what happened that morning in Tunguska?

The first scientists didn't reach the site until 1927. Russia was in political chaos after the revolution, and the region was almost impossible to reach. When the expedition finally arrived, led by mineralogist Leonid Kulik, they were stunned. The devastation was still visible nearly 20 years later.

Eighty million trees had been knocked over in a radial pattern. Some were burned at the top but untouched at the base—suggesting intense heat from above. Others were left standing, their limbs stripped clean. But at ground zero, Kulik found no crater. No debris. No obvious source.

Villagers from hundreds of miles away reported seeing a column of blue light moving across the sky, followed by a fiery flash and waves of hot air. One man said he was thrown from his chair. Another said he saw the trees "burning from the inside."

Seismic stations around the world had picked up the blast. It registered like an earthquake—one strong enough to be felt as far away as Britain.

At first, people guessed it was a meteor strike. But without a crater, it didn't fit the usual model. Others thought it was a volcanic explosion or an underground gas eruption. But there were no volcanoes nearby. And gas couldn't explain the shockwave.

In the decades that followed, dozens of theories piled up.

One popular explanation is that a small asteroid or comet entered Earth's atmosphere at high speed—then exploded mid-air before hitting the ground. This kind of event is called an airburst, and it's been modeled using computer simulations. The fireball would have released energy equal to 10 to 15 megatons of TNT—hundreds of times more powerful than the atomic bomb dropped on Hiroshima.

If true, that would explain the heat, the flattened trees, and the lack of a crater. But it still leaves open questions.

For one, no fragments have ever been conclusively identified. Comets are made mostly of ice and dust, and they might not leave behind much—but an asteroid should've left traces. Some small pieces have been found in nearby peat bogs, but none are large enough to confirm the source.

In the 1970s and 80s, researchers suggested another possibility: a comet made of mostly frozen gas, which would have vaporized completely upon entering the atmosphere.

That would leave behind minimal debris—just air, light, and an invisible hammer blow.

But the theories didn't stop there.

In later years, more outlandish ideas began to circulate: a miniature black hole had passed through the Earth. A fragment of antimatter had collided with our atmosphere. A secret weapons test had gone wrong. Or even that an alien spacecraft had exploded mid-flight.

There's no evidence for any of those claims. But the lack of closure kept the speculation alive.

More recently, scientists have pointed to other airbursts—like the one over Chelyabinsk, Russia in 2013—as a comparison. That meteor exploded high in the atmosphere, injured over a thousand people, and shattered windows across a city. It left no crater, but fragments were recovered. The Tunguska Event may have been a much larger version of the same thing.

Today, the blast zone has regrown into forest, but the trees still grow in strange directions. Satellite images show the same radial pattern left behind in 1908. Visitors still report an eerie silence at the center.

We know something exploded. We know it came from above. We know the energy release was massive.

What we don't know is exactly what object caused it—or whether it left anything behind that we've simply missed.

No crater. No wreckage. Just a wound in the trees, a spike in the seismic record, and one quiet morning that ended in a flash of heat and sky.

THE
ROSWELL UFO
INCIDENT

What really happened that summer in
Roswell, New Mexico?

Could the truth still be hidden, locked away in
some government vault?

The rancher didn't know what to make of it.

On July 5, 1947, a man named Mac Brazel discovered strange debris scattered across his pasture near Roswell, New Mexico. Shiny fragments were embedded in the ground. Some were paper-thin but wouldn't tear, burn, or bend. Others looked like small metal beams, impossibly light and covered in symbols he couldn't read.

He had never seen anything like it.

Two days later, he brought the material to the local sheriff, who contacted the nearby Roswell Army Air Field. Soldiers arrived quickly. They cordoned off the area, collected the debris, and told Brazel not to talk about what he'd found.

The next day, the military made a stunning announcement: they had recovered a "flying disc."

Within hours, that story was replaced.

A new press release claimed it wasn't a flying saucer—it was a weather balloon. The original statement had been a mistake. The wreckage was part of a routine high-altitude balloon used to study weather patterns.

Case closed.

Or so they said.

But the story didn't disappear. It grew.

Over the next few years, Roswell became just another Cold War footnote. Then, in the late 1970s, researchers tracked down several military personnel who had been stationed at Roswell during the incident. Some claimed the original debris was not from any known aircraft. A few said they had seen bodies—small, humanoid, and not from this world.

That's when the Roswell Incident took on a new life.

Witness accounts surfaced describing a second crash site, further from the ranch, where another craft had allegedly gone down. A mortician said he was asked to provide child-sized coffins. A nurse claimed she'd seen an autopsy on something that wasn't human. Others described crates of wreckage being flown out under heavy guard.

No photos. No documents. Just testimony.

The U.S. government maintained the balloon explanation. But questions kept coming.

In 1994, nearly fifty years after the incident, the U.S. Air Force issued a new report: the debris had been part of Project Mogul, a top-secret program using high-altitude balloons to detect Soviet nuclear tests. The materials found—metallic strips, rubber, sticks—were consistent with balloon payloads. The secrecy, they said, was to avoid revealing military technology during the Cold War.

As for the bodies? The 1997 follow-up report claimed those were dummies used in high-altitude parachute tests— though those tests were conducted years after the Roswell crash.

By then, the story had already gone global.

Roswell was no longer just a location—it was a symbol. The site of a possible cover-up. The place where, many believed, the government had its first contact with something extraterrestrial and chose to hide the truth.

TV specials, books, conventions, and documentaries poured in. Eyewitnesses were tracked down, interviewed, challenged, and defended. The more time passed, the harder it became to separate fact from belief.

Skeptics point out that memories fade, details shift, and stories often grow with retelling. Some accounts contradict each other. Many surfaced decades after the event.

But there are also details that remain hard to dismiss.

Why did the military first announce the recovery of a flying disc—then change the story within a single day?

Why were soldiers sent in so quickly, and why was the debris transported to multiple bases across the country?

Why did witnesses describe materials that modern technology still struggles to explain?

And why were official explanations rewritten nearly fifty years after the fact?

The lack of physical evidence means Roswell may never be fully resolved. No confirmed photos. No samples available for testing. No written logs that match the claims of alien recovery.

Just conflicting press releases. A lot of questions. And decades of debate.

We know something crashed in the New Mexico desert in July of 1947.

We know the military handled it with unusual speed and secrecy.

We know that over time, the event shifted—from local oddity to global legend.

And we know that when it comes to Roswell, what people believe often matters more than what they can prove.

Not because the evidence is clear. But because the trail never really went cold.

MOTHMAN

What exactly is the Mothman? Is it
a real creature with flesh and blood,
or could it be some kind of ghostly
figure that crosses into our world
from somewhere else?

Why does it only show up before
something terrible happens?

It had wings.

That much, everyone agreed on.

The night was November 15, 1966. Two young couples were driving near an old TNT plant outside Point Pleasant, West Virginia, when their headlights swept over a shape on the road.

Tall. Human-shaped. But wrong.

Its eyes glowed red.

Its wings unfurled.

And when they turned the car around, it followed—lifting off the ground without a sound, gliding low, fast, and silent.

The chase ended back in town. The witnesses were pale, trembling, insistent. They'd seen something they couldn't explain.

They weren't the last.

Let's examine the evidence.

Over the next year, dozens of people in Point Pleasant reported seeing the same thing: a winged figure, six to seven feet tall, with glowing red eyes and a massive wingspan. Some said it hovered over cars. Others claimed it appeared outside their windows. Many were scared to speak up—until the local press gave the creature a name:

Mothman.

That's clue #1: multiple sightings, from people with no reason to lie.

The descriptions weren't identical, but they rhymed: wings like a bat, eyes like tail lights, and a feeling—described again and again—of overwhelming dread.

Then the second wave of strangeness began.

Lights in the sky. Malfunctioning electronics. Phone calls with strange static or robotic voices. Some residents reported being followed or questioned by men in black suits—who knew things they shouldn't.

And all of it seemed to orbit one location: the old munitions plant on the edge of town.

An abandoned WWII site with tunnels, bunkers, and decay. Locals said it was cursed. Or contaminated. Or both.

Clue #2: the sightings clustered around a single place—and then stopped.

On December 15, 1967, tragedy struck.

The Silver Bridge, which connected Point Pleasant to Ohio, collapsed during rush hour. Forty-six people died. No warning. Just steel snapping like twigs and cars tumbling into the icy river.

After that, the Mothman vanished.

Some said it was a coincidence. Others believed the creature was a warning—a prophetic sign of doom. A few claimed to see it again, just before other disasters: the Chernobyl meltdown, the I-35 bridge collapse in Minnesota, the Fukushima earthquake.

Maybe it doesn't cause tragedy. Maybe it *appears* when disaster is near.

Clue #3: the pattern isn't just sightings—it's timing.

So what is it?

Skeptics offer explanations. They say it was likely a misidentified animal—maybe a barred owl or a sandhill crane. The red eyes? Light reflecting off the retina. The wings? Just the mind filling in details in the dark.

Fear, after all, is a powerful lens.

Others think it was mass hysteria. One scary story grows legs, then wings. People see what they expect to see.

But that doesn't explain the bridge. Or the fact that, after the collapse, the sightings stopped cold.

More fringe theories emerged. Some believe the Mothman is an alien. A dimensional traveler. A tulpa—a creature born from collective belief. Or an omen, like the banshees of old folklore: not evil, but unavoidable. A signal.

A shadow falling ahead of catastrophe.

Then there's the evidence that isn't evidence—no photos that hold up under scrutiny. No feathers, no footprints. Just testimony. Just memory.

But memory is powerful.

In Point Pleasant today, there's a museum. A statue. An annual festival. But beneath the tourist fun is something quieter—a community that remembers fear. Real fear. That strange year where things in the sky didn't make sense, and something with wings refused to follow the rules of the natural world.

The case isn't solved. Maybe it never will be.

But here's the final clue:

Not all mysteries leave proof.

Some just leave people behind who can't stop looking up.

THE OAKVILLE BLOBS

What could cause strange, jelly-like
blobs to fall from the sky?

Was it a freak accident of nature, or
something from another world?

ugust 7, 1994. 3:00 a.m. Oakville, Washington. Population: around 600.

It started as rain.

But not the kind that trickles off rooftops. This came down in blobs—gelatinous, colorless, and strangely silent. By morning, it coated yards, streets, barns, and car windshields. Locals said it felt like Jell-O. Some poked it with sticks. Others touched it barehanded.

It happened again. And again. Six times over three weeks.

Then people started getting sick.

Officer David Lacey was on patrol that first night when his windshield smeared with goo. The wipers made it worse. At a gas station, while trying to clean it off, he felt lightheaded. Dizzy. Hours later, both he and the attendant were violently ill—nausea, vertigo, trouble breathing.

They weren't alone. Dozens of Oakville residents reported flu-like symptoms. Some lasted days. Some, weeks. A few, months.

Then came the animals. One woman, Dotty Hearn, stepped outside to examine the strange rain. She collapsed in her home hours later. Her cats and dogs, exposed to the blobs, got sick. One kitten died.

Doctors found low blood pressure, dehydration, and inner ear issues—but no clear cause.

Samples were sent to labs. The Washington State Department of Health reported human white blood cells. Another lab found two types of bacteria—one found in the human gut.

It wasn't chemical. It wasn't pollen. It was biological.

But not blue ice from a plane. FAA ruled that out. Aircraft waste is dyed, smelly, and doesn't fall cleanly from the sky. These blobs were odorless and oddly precise.

So where did they come from?

One theory: jellyfish.

Military exercises had taken place off the coast days before. Could an explosion have launched jellyfish into the atmosphere?

It sounds absurd—but locals saw aircraft. Not just jets. Unmarked helicopters. Low passes. No answers.

The jellyfish idea hit the news—but scientists pointed out problems. Jellyfish don't contain human white blood cells. And they wouldn't stay intact through freezing altitudes.

So that theory sank.

Another idea: a test gone wrong.

Some believe Oakville was part of a classified experiment—perhaps involving bacteria dispersal, weather control, or biowarfare. Cloaked as "weird weather."

But there's no proof. No documents. Just timing. And silence.

In 1997, Unsolved Mysteries aired a segment on the Oakville blobs. Public interest exploded. New samples were re-tested. Some microbiologists claimed to find cells with nuclei—meaning it wasn't bacteria, but something more complex.

Others said the samples had degraded too far to tell.

Eventually, the blobs stopped. The symptoms faded. But the questions stayed.

And in Oakville, people remember.

The strange jelly on the porch. The pets that never recovered. The helicopters. The lack of answers.

Some mysteries leave behind ancient carvings or stone ruins. Others? Just a smear on your windshield. A fever. And the sense that someone knows more than they're saying.

Whatever fell that night?

It wasn't just rain.

AREA 51

What really happens behind the fences of Area 51? Is it all just top-secret military stuff, or could it actually involve aliens and UFOs?

Why is the government so secretive about it?

REVERSE ENGINEERING
— PROJECT: XENO

For decades, it didn't appear on any map.

No flight paths crossed it. No records acknowledged it. No satellite images showed it. The name "Area 51" was never spoken by officials. Reporters asking about it received blank stares or nervous laughs.

And yet it had fences, gates, patrols, and motion sensors. Satellite dishes. Aircraft hangars. Security clearances so high that even generals didn't have access.

The U.S. government said nothing.

Then came the clues.

First were the maps that had holes. Sections blacked out. Regions labeled "Restricted Airspace" with no explanation. Pilots told not to fly over. Radar dead zones in the middle of the Nevada desert.

Then came the workers. Scientists, engineers, and military contractors who traveled in each morning from Las Vegas on unmarked planes—white jets with no logos, no flight numbers, and one known destination: Groom Lake.

That's the real name. Groom Lake. A dry lakebed north of Las Vegas, near the Nellis Test Range. But the world knows it by a different name: Area 51.

In 1955, something new appeared on the lakebed—a long, flat runway and a few sheds. That same year, test flights began for a new spy plane called the U-2, designed to fly at 70,000 feet to photograph Soviet missile sites. It was a top-secret program run by the CIA.

And that was the beginning.

Over the next few decades, Area 51 became a testing ground for experimental aircraft: the A-12 Oxcart, which flew three times the speed of sound. The D-21 drone. The F-117 Nighthawk, one of the first stealth planes. All developed and tested under deep secrecy, often decades before the public learned they existed.

That's what made the cover-up so effective.

If people saw something strange flying overhead—something shaped like a triangle, or a teardrop, or a black arrow—they weren't seeing a UFO. They were seeing tomorrow's technology in today's skies.

At least, that's what the official line says now.

But the UFO reports didn't stop. In fact, they grew.

In the 1980s, a man named Bob Lazar claimed to have worked at a site near Area 51, reverse-engineering alien spacecraft. He described hangars built into the mountainside, nine flying saucers, and a reactor powered by a mysterious element no one had ever heard of: Element 115.

His story was dismissed by scientists, but he passed multiple lie detector tests. His security clearance couldn't be confirmed—but neither could it be disproven. And he knew details about the base's layout that no one had published before.

That's when Area 51 became more than a military site. It became a symbol.

A place where aliens were stored.

Where bodies were autopsied.

Where spacecraft were rebuilt.

Where truth was buried under a hundred layers of red tape.

In 2013, the CIA finally acknowledged the existence of Area 51—on paper. They released declassified documents showing that yes, the base existed, and yes, it had been used for secret aircraft development. But no mention was made of extraterrestrial craft, alien bodies, or anything beyond the scope of military technology.

For some, that ended the debate.

For others, it only proved that the government was still hiding more than it admitted.

Because the strangest part isn't the technology. It's the layers of silence.

Over 70 years, no journalist has ever been allowed inside the base. Photos are forbidden. Airspace remains restricted. Workers are flown in and out on daily classified flights. No one ever speaks on the record. And those who do are quickly discredited—or discredited themselves.

Visitors to the edge of the site describe white pickup trucks parked on distant hillsides, watching silently. Warning signs threaten arrest, imprisonment, or worse. Cameras track every movement.

So what is Area 51?

A test site? A vault? A story built around denial?

We know what's been admitted: spy planes, stealth jets, cutting-edge tech.

We know what's been claimed: flying discs, alien bodies, secret physics.

But the real mystery may not be what's there. It's how many versions of the truth have been layered over it.

Official programs covered by secret ones.
Myths masking experiments.
And silence so deep it becomes part of the structure itself.

Area 51 is no longer a single mystery. It's a map made of blacked-out lines.

And every one of them leads somewhere you're not allowed to go.

D.B. COOPER

What really happened to D.B. Cooper after he jumped into the night sky?

What about the ransom cash— where did it go, and why was only a small portion of it ever found?

I HAVE A BOMB

He gave his name as Dan Cooper.

It was the day before Thanksgiving—November 24, 1971. He was calm, well-dressed, polite. A dark suit, a black tie with a mother-of-pearl clip, a neatly combed part. He looked like a businessman boarding a short flight from Portland to Seattle.

It was a 30-minute trip on Northwest Orient Flight 305. There were 36 passengers. Nothing unusual.

Then Cooper handed a note to the flight attendant.

She assumed it was a phone number. He leaned in and whispered, "Miss, you'd better read that. I have a bomb."

Inside his briefcase, he showed her wires and red sticks. The note demanded $200,000 in cash, four parachutes, and a fuel truck ready in Seattle. If his demands weren't met, he would blow up the plane.

The airline and the FBI agreed. When the plane landed, Cooper let the passengers go. The money and parachutes were delivered. He kept the crew aboard and ordered the pilots to take off again—heading south toward Mexico City, flying low and slow.

Then, somewhere over the thick forests of Washington state, he jumped.

He opened the rear staircase mid-flight, stepped out into the cold November night, and disappeared.

No one ever saw him again.

The FBI scrambled. They launched one of the largest manhunts in U.S. history. Helicopters, military aircraft, and ground teams searched the suspected drop zone near the Lewis River.

But they found nothing.

No body. No parachute. No clear trace of the man calling himself Dan Cooper.

The only evidence he left behind was on the plane: a black clip-on tie, eight cigarette butts (long since lost), and 66 unidentified fingerprints.

In the days that followed, agents traced the parachutes and marked the ransom bills with serial numbers. The name "Dan Cooper" turned out to be fake, though newspapers mistakenly called him "D.B. Cooper"—a typo that stuck.

The most basic questions couldn't be answered.

Who was he? Where did he land? Did he survive?

Some thought he was a skilled paratrooper or military pilot. But experts pointed out flaws: he jumped into a storm, in the dark, over rugged terrain. He wore loafers and a trench coat. He rejected a military-grade parachute in favor of a non-steerable training chute. Not smart choices for someone planning to live.

Others believed he didn't survive. The woods were dangerous. The river was freezing. If he had died on impact, animals or weather could have erased the evidence.

Then, nearly a decade later, a new clue surfaced.

In 1980, a boy digging on the banks of the Columbia River found three bundles of cash. They matched the serial numbers of the ransom money. The bills were rotted and scattered—but they hadn't been buried. Just… lodged in the sand, as if placed there or washed in by the river.

The find was 20 miles west of the drop zone—nowhere near where Cooper was expected to land.

This changed the search again. But no other money ever turned up. Not in circulation, not in caches, not even by metal detector sweeps of the site.

Over the next 50 years, more than 800 suspects were investigated.

One was a former paratrooper with a history of skydiving. One was a commercial airline pilot. One claimed to be Cooper on his deathbed—then recanted. Another matched the physical description and had once told a friend, "There's something you should know, but I can't tell you."

In 2016, the FBI officially closed the case. No charges. No arrest. No name. Just a case file marked UNSOLVED.

The Cooper hijacking remains the only unsolved skyjacking in U.S. history.

The FBI has Cooper's DNA from his tie, but no match. They have the serial numbers of the bills, but no trail. They have radar data from that night, but no certainty about where he jumped.

All they ever had were guesses.

Was he a desperate man with nothing to lose?

A brilliant planner who vanished into a new life?

A myth in the making, born the moment his boots left the stairwell?

The cash is mostly gone. The evidence is cold. The man is still missing.

And the only thing that ever left a mark... was the jump.

WOW! SIGNAL

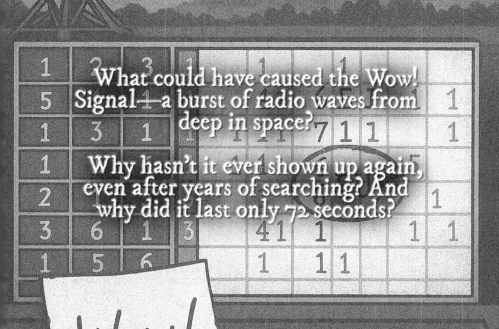

What could have caused the Wow! Signal—a burst of radio waves from deep in space?

Why hasn't it ever shown up again, even after years of searching? And why did it last only 72 seconds?

Wow!

The telescope wasn't even aiming at anything in particular.

It was part of a long, patient scan—an automated project known as SETI, the Search for Extraterrestrial Intelligence. Night after night, the Big Ear radio telescope at Ohio State University listened to deep space, hoping for a signal that didn't sound like nature.

And on August 15, 1977, something called back.

A narrowband radio transmission—loud, focused, and lasting 72 seconds—came through at 1420 MHz, the frequency of hydrogen. It was exactly the kind of signal SETI had been trained to detect.

Not a hum. Not a burst of static.

A clear spike in data, far stronger than background noise. So strong that volunteer astronomer Jerry Ehman circled the data on the printout and scribbled a single word in the margin:

Wow!

Let's follow the clues.

Clue #1: the frequency.

1420 MHz is significant. It's the natural emission line of hydrogen—the most common element in the universe. Many scientists believed that any alien civilization broadcasting a signal would choose that frequency to increase the odds of it being noticed. If someone wanted to be heard, this is where they'd speak.

Clue #2: the structure.

The Wow! Signal wasn't random. It followed a pattern—a smooth rise and fall in intensity, like something passing across the telescope's field of view. That ruled out local interference or a brief glitch. It looked like a real astronomical source.

Clue #3: it never came back.

Follow-up scans were made. Over and over. Dozens of telescopes tried to find the signal again. It never reappeared. Never repeated. Never explained.

That's what makes it so maddening.

It wasn't a hoax. It wasn't a known satellite. It wasn't any natural cosmic event we could identify. It was a single, clean voice in the void—and then silence.

Some thought it might have been a military transmission bouncing off space debris. Others speculated it could be a comet's hydrogen cloud. But no explanation has stuck. Each has been tested and ruled out—or left unproven.

Today, the Wow! Signal remains the best candidate ever detected for extraterrestrial contact.

It lasted just over a minute.

That's it.

No reply. No coordinates. No message.

Just one moment when the numbers on a computer readout changed—and suggested we weren't listening alone.

Maybe it was just space being weird.

Or maybe it was someone waving back.

DANCING STONES
OF DEATH VALLEY

How could massive rocks move on
their own?

Is it magic, some kind of mysterious
energy, or maybe a trick of nature?

T he stones had moved.

Not rolled, not tumbled. Glided.

Across a dry lakebed in the middle of Death Valley—one of the hottest, most desolate places on Earth—rocks had left trails in the cracked mud. Long, looping tracks, like someone had dragged them slowly across the ground. But there were no people. No machines. No footprints.

And the rocks were heavy.

Some weighed over 600 pounds.

They had no reason to move. But they did.

That was the mystery of Racetrack Playa.

You can see the trails with your own eyes. They stretch for dozens of feet, sometimes curved, sometimes perfectly straight. Some tracks run parallel. Others crisscross or double back on themselves. The stones rest at the ends of the trails like they'd just stopped to catch their breath.

Locals had noticed them for decades. Cowboys. Park rangers. Geologists. Everyone agreed something strange was happening out on the playa—but no one could say exactly what.

Because no one had ever seen it happen.

That was clue #1: the rocks moved—but only when no one was looking.

Some people blamed powerful winds. Others guessed it had something to do with freezing temperatures, rare rainfall, or even magnetic anomalies. A few simply called it a natural illusion—tracks formed by some geological fluke, misunderstood by casual observers.

Still, the puzzle stuck.

Scientists knew Racetrack Playa could flood after rare desert rains. Thin sheets of water would pool over the dry lakebed, then evaporate in the sun. But that didn't explain the tracks—not completely. The surface was too flat. The stones too large. The marks too deliberate.

So researchers started watching.

In the 1970s, a geologist named Robert Sharp launched a long-term study. He marked individual stones with flags and monitored them for years. Some moved. Others didn't. There was no clear pattern—just slow, silent shifts that left behind unmistakable trails.

The mystery deepened.

Then, in 2013, the breakthrough came—not with a storm, but with patience.

A pair of researchers, Richard and Jim Norris, installed time-lapse cameras and GPS trackers on several stones. For months, nothing happened. Then came a rare combination: rain followed by a deep overnight freeze, and then sun.

And just like that, the stones danced.

Thin sheets of ice had formed beneath a shallow layer of water. As the sun rose, the ice cracked into panels that floated on the water's surface. A steady breeze pushed the ice—and the ice pushed the rocks.

The movement was slow, barely visible. But it was real.

Stones the size of microwaves, drifting across the desert on their own.

That was clue #2: nature had an answer—but it was stranger than fiction.

The ice wasn't lifting the rocks. It was guiding them. The mud beneath, saturated and soft, recorded each motion like a signature in wet cement.

For decades, people had assumed the stones moved all at once, maybe in violent storms. In reality, they slid inches at a time under the quiet power of wind and thawing ice.

Not supernatural. Not magnetic. Just unlikely.

But here's the thing:

Knowing how it happens doesn't make it less weird.

Because when you stand out on Racetrack Playa, surrounded by silence and cracked earth, it still doesn't feel like it should be possible.

You don't see the wind. You don't see the ice. You just see the trails—and the stones.

Resting. Waiting.

Some researchers still debate the exact details. Not all tracks are alike. Some curves are too sharp, some paths too erratic. Could there be more than one force at work? Could some tracks be older, formed under different conditions?

The ice theory solved the mystery for some. But not all.

And no one has filmed the larger rocks moving. Only the small and mid-sized ones.

That's clue #3: even when you have part of the answer, parts of the question remain.

So what do we call it?

A solved mystery?

A slow-motion miracle?

A geological sleight of hand?

Maybe it's all of those.

Because sometimes, a rock sliding across the desert is more than a rock.

It's a reminder that the Earth still does things we don't expect. Slowly. Quietly. Without anyone watching.

And if you happen to walk out there at just the right moment—and the ice is thin, and the wind just steady enough—you might catch one of them in motion.

THE
PHOENIX
LIGHTS

What could have caused the strange
lights in the sky above Phoenix?

How could something so huge
move so quietly and in such perfect
formation?

No sound. No wind. No blinking lights.

Just five glowing orbs, hovering in a perfect V.

On the night of March 13, 1997, thousands of people across Arizona looked up and saw something they couldn't explain. The event would stretch for more than three hours, cover over 300 miles, and become one of the most well-documented mass UFO sightings in history.

It's known today as the Phoenix Lights.

The first calls came in around 7:55 p.m., near Henderson, Nevada. A man reported a large object in the sky with six lights in a V formation, moving silently and slowly. He said it was "the size of a 747." No engine noise. No strobe.

Minutes later, people in Paulden, Prescott, and Dewey, Arizona began reporting the same thing. Witnesses described a massive triangular craft, blotting out stars as it passed overhead. Some said it was low enough to see the structure itself. Others said the lights were all they could make out.

By the time it reached Phoenix just after 10:00 p.m., the lights had formed a huge V shape moving silently over the city. Drivers pulled over. Families stood in backyards. News stations started taking calls.

One former police officer described the object as "a mile wide, minimum."

A family playing basketball said it passed directly over them—black, silent, and so low it felt like it could land on the street.

Not everyone saw the exact same thing. Some described orbs. Some saw a solid craft. Some said the lights moved independently, others swore they were fixed to a single structure. But the time, shape, and path were consistent.

Then, just as suddenly, it was gone.

And that's when the second wave began.

Around 10:30 p.m., a new formation of lights appeared near the horizon south of Phoenix—this time in a straight line. They hovered for minutes, then disappeared one by one.

The military quickly claimed the second sighting was flares dropped by aircraft during a training exercise at Luke Air Force Base. But that didn't explain what people had seen earlier—hundreds of miles of reports from people of all ages, professions, and backgrounds.

The Phoenix Lights weren't just strange—they were coordinated.

There was no radar confirmation of a large craft. No FAA warnings. No military admission of an aircraft fitting that description.

Governor Fife Symington, then Arizona's top official, initially held a press conference poking fun at the reports—bringing out an aide in an alien costume. But years later, he changed his story. He said he had seen the lights himself and believed it was "otherworldly." He claimed the object was massive, solid, and silent.

The Air Force later stated that no unusual activity occurred that night, beyond the flare drop. But the timing didn't add up. The flares came after the citywide reports. And flares don't move in formation for 100 miles. They drift. They flicker. They fall.

Some tried to explain the lights as aircraft flying in military formation, but FAA officials confirmed that no planes were scheduled along that flight path. And again, none of the witnesses reported hearing engines or jet noise.

Others blamed weather balloons, reflections, or mass misidentification. But multiple commercial pilots, police officers, and air traffic controllers were among those who saw the event. They didn't all agree on what it was—but they knew what it wasn't.

One of the most puzzling things about the Phoenix Lights is how quiet it was. Thousands of people saw it. Hundreds called in. But there was no panic, no traffic chaos, no widespread alarm. Just people staring up—confused, curious, unsure.

To this day, no confirmed photos or videos exist of the original V-shaped object, only of the later flare formation. This adds to the confusion. The most bizarre part of the sighting left behind the least physical evidence—just witness drawings, interviews, and recordings of frantic calls to news stations.

The lights returned briefly in 2007 and 2008, sparking new interest—but those were quickly confirmed as flares.

The 1997 event remains unsolved.

The government doesn't classify it as a UFO incident. No craft has been recovered. No official explanation has addressed both waves of sightings. And no footage has surfaced showing the object as clearly as the people beneath it did.

A shape in the sky. A city paused in silence. A list of reports that reads like a chorus.

There was something up there.

Too slow to be a jet.

Too large to be a drone.

Too coordinated to be chance.

And for one night in Arizona, the sky didn't behave the way it was supposed to.

AFTERWORD

The Mystery Never Ends

So… what do you think?

After all the pyramids, lost cities, coded messages, vanishing ships, and unexplainable artifacts—what's your theory? Did you find a favorite mystery? A clue that didn't fit? A theory you think everyone else missed?

Here's the thing about real-world mysteries: they don't always wrap up with a perfect ending. There's no final boss, no big reveal, no neat conclusion. Not yet.

Because history is still being uncovered. New technology is scanning what the eye can't see. Divers are still finding strange shapes on the seafloor. Hikers stumble across ancient carvings. Satellites spot forgotten ruins from space. The puzzle never stops growing.

But neither do the clues.

Someone still has to connect them. Someone curious. Someone determined. Someone willing to say, "Wait— that doesn't make sense," and then dig deeper.

Why not you?

Maybe you'll be the one to finally translate the Voynich Manuscript. Or figure out what the Big Void in the Great Pyramid was really used for. Or solve the mystery of the dancing stones in Death Valley. Maybe you'll create a theory no one else has thought of. Or prove one wrong.

What matters is how you think.

Do you follow the evidence? Question your own ideas? Notice what others ignore?

That's how real discoveries are made—not by guessing, but by investigating.

The stories in this book may be ancient. But the search is just beginning.

So stay curious. Stay sharp. Keep asking the weird questions.

Because the clues are still out there.

And the next one?

It might be yours to find.

Yours,

Rex Langley

PLEASE LEAVE A REVIEW

You've unraveled history's strangest mysteries... but one last secret remains:

How did you like the book?

Your quick review would mean the world –and it helps others discover their next mystery!

BERMUDA TRIANGLE

Made in the USA
Coppell, TX
27 June 2025